Uncivil Liberties

Deconstructing Libertarianism

Uncivil Liberties

Deconstructing Libertarianism

GEORGIA KELLY
Co-Author and Editor

BEN BOYCE, BENJAMIN "NICK" COLBY,
GUS DiZEREGA, JULIANNE E. MAURSETH,
and BARRY SPECTOR
Co-Authors

Foreword by Hazel Henderson

PRAXIS PEACE INSTITUTE
Sonoma & New York

Text design by Maria E. Torres | helenpr66@gmail.com.
Cover design by www.popshopstudio.com.
Cover illustration © istockphoto.com/ #21639298

ISBN: 978-0-98861-3-003

Ordering Information:
Praxis publications are available at online bookstores. They may also be purchased for educational, business, or promotional use:
Bulk orders: Special discounts are available on bulk orders for reading groups, organizations, businesses, and others.
Custom-label orders: We offer selected books with your customized cover or logo of choice.

For more information, contact us at:

Praxis Peace Institute
P.O. Box 416, Old Chelsea Station
New York, NY 10011

praxis@cosimobooks.com
www.praxispeace.org

CONTENTS

Acknowledgments • vii

Foreword by Hazel Henderson • ix

Introduction • xiii

CHAPTER 1

The Mythic Foundations of American Libertarianism • 1

By Barry Spector

CHAPTER 2

The Individual and Civil Society • 27

By Georgia Kelly

CHAPTER 3

Transcendental Vanilla Pudding • 46

By Ben Boyce

CHAPTER 4

Turning the Tables:

The Pathologies and Unrealized Promise of Libertarianism • 56

By Gus diZerega

CHAPTER 5

How Libertarianism Seduces Americans Away from Democracy • 113

By Julianne E. Maurseth

CHAPTER 6

Defining Ideologies with a Cultural Compass • 148

By Benjamin "Nick" Colby

About the Authors • 187

About Praxis Peace Institute • 191

ACKNOWLEDGMENTS

THIS PROJECT EMERGED from the Praxis Peace Institute Book Club and has been a wonderful collaboration from start to finish. As editor of this book and director of Praxis Peace Institute, I want to thank the authors, as they have donated time in researching and writing their respective chapters. It has been a labor of love filled with enthusiasm.

The authors (collectively) would like to thank people who helped with this effort from the earliest to the final stages. They are Philip Beard, Moira Brennan, Dan Drasin, Susan Fegan, Amy Petersen, and Dave Ransom, who proofed and edited some of the early copy for the pamphlet, "Deconstructing Libertarianism," which was the precursor to this book. Thanks also to Tom McKean for putting the pieces together in the original pamphlet and to all the above for making sense of our process.

We must thank Foster and Kimberly Gamble, who created the film *Thrive* and its accompanying website, for motivating us to respond from a progressive perspective. Though we differ greatly in our solutions, we identify some of the same problems facing humanity today.

We would like to also acknowledge moral support from authors Duane Elgin, Elisabet Sahtouris, and John Robbins, who confirmed the necessity of responding to the *Thrive* film and website.

We are grateful to Swami Beyondananda (aka Steve Bhaerman) for coming up with our title, *Uncivil Liberties*, which captures the essence of our critique.

We also extend a special thanks to economist and author Hazel Henderson for supporting this endeavor from pamphlet to book and for suggesting our publisher, Cosimo Books. We are forever grateful to you. As editor, I appreciate the conversations and email exchanges we had during the writing of this book.

Other long-time supporters of and specific contributors to Praxis Peace Institute who made a publication like this possible are the Firedoll Foundation, the Appleby Foundation, Faye and Sandor Straus, Chandra and Robert Friese, David and Lila Tresemer, Howard and Jean Fenton, Joanie Misrak Ciardelli, Shaula Massena, and Donald M. Davis. We deeply appreciate your support and belief in our work.

We would like to thank the staff at Cosimo Books, especially editor Katherine Mason, who have contributed to the manifestation of this book with enthusiasm, attention to detail, and continual helpfulness. As it turns out, Praxis Peace Institute already had a connection with Cosimo. In the summer of 2007, Cosimo's founder and publisher, Alex Dake, attended a Praxis conference in Dubrovnik, Croatia. So working together to publish this book has been a warm and welcome reunion. Our deepest appreciation goes to Alex for understanding and encouraging our project from the first meeting.

Georgia Kelly
Director, Praxis Peace Institute

FOREWORD

I WELCOME *UNCIVIL LIBERTIES* as a sobering wake-up call to my beloved adopted country, the USA, and its people. We are, I believe, in the midst of a whole-system global transition from the past 300 years of fossil-fueled industrialism and expansion to the biological and ecological realities of our finite planet. These realities include accepting that we humans are one among thirty million other species inhabiting our biosphere and all exist and thrive on the daily flow of free photons from our Mother Star: the Sun. Indeed, we at Ethical Markets Media, which I founded in 2004 to reform markets and metrics while growing cleaner, greener, knowledge-rich economies, address these biological realities in "Transforming Finance Based on Ethics and Life's Principles," a paper co-developed with our partners at the Biomimicry Institute.

This great global transition now underway signals the end of GDP-measured industrial expansion and illustrates the errors at the core of economics that permitted this single-minded focus on maximizing private profit by "externalizing" social and environmental costs to others. All these false ideologies were de-frocked in the financial crises of 2008 and the bailouts of their perpetrators.

The authors of *Uncivil Liberties* de-mystify the social and cultural myths and religious beliefs that underpin the still prevailing economic fundamentalism that drove corporate executives, Wall Street traders, central bankers, and compliant politicians into denial. Their efforts led them to further inflate un-repayable levels of debt by giving printed money to insolvent too-big-to-fail corporations. They were abetted by the Supreme Court's 2010 decision that these legal abstractions, originally chartered by governments for the public good, were freed from such obligations since they were defined as "persons" with the full rights of citizens, but with fewer obligations and limited liability.

This book and the deeply insightful perspectives of its co-authors help us understand how all these travesties could have happened and why they are still occurring. In examining the premises of libertarianism and its deep roots in the history and culture of the polarized but still united States of America, they plumb the deepest conflicts in all human societies: the individual versus the group. We learn how the myths of the frontier, the rugged individuals celebrated by the Horatio Alger and Ayn Rand stories, came to dominate our politics and economy—reinforced by commercial advertising and peer pressure to "keep up with the Joneses." As corporate money captured politicians, it channeled aspirations away from service for the common good to heroic feats of consumption. I explored the psychology and resulting personal anxieties of all this in my article titled "The End of Jonesism" (*The Futurist*, 1975).

I became a U.S. citizen in 1961 and at first was entranced by this cult of individualism—so different from my upbringing in Britain where group and community bonds still predominate. I read Ayn Rand's novels and identified with her hero John Galt, sympathizing with her obvious overreaction to life under the Soviet Union's totalitarianism. I also understand her appeal to adolescents and mostly males of all ages, from hedge fund and private-equity players to former Fed Chairman Alan Greenspan and recent vice-presidential candidate Paul Ryan, both of whom are devotees.

For me, reality overtook my adolescent escapism. I became a mother, and saw how the pollution of New York City's air was harming my baby as she played with others in soot-covered sandboxes in an urban play park shadowed by a vast Con Edison power plant. As I learned the ropes of becoming a U.S. citizen, I co-founded Citizens for Clean Air in 1964 with the other mothers in that play park. It wasn't long before I realized the problem of pollution was encouraged by economic textbooks that claimed air and water as "free" for the taking, that rational human behavior was self-interested and competitive against all others, that money was equated with wealth and that this money-denominated view of success was encoded into GNP as national "progress"! I was horrified and determined to find out what else was wrong with economics, which led to a lifelong crusade and is a theme in all my books.

Georgia Kelly is the kind of inspired community activist I admire—with deep scholarship grounding her mature wisdom and passion for the common good. We connect deeply in our vision for humanity's evolution toward wisdom, maturity, and responsibility at the planetary level—to create just, peaceful societies based on deep respect for all life. Georgia works on the deepest levels in fostering peace—including editing and authoring *Uncivil Liberties* and, with her co-authors, unraveling the depths of U.S. culture and politics. This deep level is now essential in leading us out of our cultural confusion, overriding the denial, the commercial censorship of all the viable alternatives and cleaner, greener technologies. The issue is not about growth versus no-growth, but as in all life, it is about what is growing, what is dying, and what should be maintained. The good news is that this green transition is underway!

All the co-authors of this book explore the myths that now must be unraveled if we are to have the coherent public debate necessary to grasp the new planetary realities. We humans now have the power to change the planet's climate, or to create deserts and floods while our unchecked financial casino becomes the flywheel of social and ecological destruction.

I hope *Uncivil Liberties* reaches the widest possible audience, both in the USA and worldwide. The world's people await our culture's maturation from adolescence to more responsible global citizenship—beyond individual human rights to our universal human responsibilities as in the Earth Charter—matching our new challenges in this Solar Age of the Anthropocene.

Hazel Henderson, D. Sc.Hon., FRSA
President, Ethical Markets Media (USA and Brazil)
www.ethicalmarkets.com
Saint Augustine, Florida
October 2012

INTRODUCTION

THOUGH ONE OF our authors says we are living in Dickensian times, I think we are also living in Orwellian times. The doublethink and newspeak written about in George Orwell's *1984* have become commonplace in media and political campaigns. The perpetual state of war that characterized Orwell's dystopia has become a reality. There is more surveillance of our activities, and propaganda has reached an all-time high in its sophistication. Unfortunately, a good public educational system that might mitigate some of the effects of propaganda has been defunded. In fact, public education has never been treated with less respect than it is today. Teachers are underpaid and their abilities questioned at every turn. Standardized testing and rote learning are given higher value than the ability to think for oneself.

Lifestyle choices are manipulated through product placement in films and television. Peer pressure to have the latest gadgets, clothes, toys, cars, houses, etc., have become common aspirations. A large segment of the population yearns to be cool, rich, famous, and even envied. Such peer manipulations were brilliantly portrayed in the film *The Joneses*, where a woman is hired to do product placement in her home and invite the neighbors over so that they too will covet and buy the furniture and gadgets displayed.

As Andrew Carnegie once said, "Capitalism is about turning luxuries into necessities." And maybe that is one of its chief problems. The planet earth cannot sustain luxurious lifestyles for everyone, or even for a fraction of its inhabitants. In understanding that we live on a finite planet with finite resources, the impetus to live responsibly has never been more needed than today, especially considering that the population is at its highest level in human history.

In assessing the political climate that currently frames the discourse, the authors of this book have decided to weigh in on the incremental dismantling of democracy we are witnessing as rightwing ideas gain in popularity. Because many Americans have a sketchy knowledge of history, they are susceptible to manipulation by ideologues with good talking points. The late Herbert Marcuse put it succinctly: "The individual's awareness of the prevailing repression is blunted by the manipulated restriction of his consciousness."[1]

Cognitive scientists George Lakoff and Drew Westen have both written about how we respond emotionally to stimuli before we engage a thought process. Propagandists understand this only too well. A strong appeal to the emotions bypasses the thought process. They know that people can be manipulated with the appropriate images, slogans, or even downright lies. By the time we stop to think about the input we receive from various media sources, we may be using our thought process to justify the slogan we just accepted as "truth." Stephen Colbert would call this type of information "truthiness." Comedian Swami Beyondananda (aka Steve Bhaerman) would call it "truth decay."

Whatever we call it, consent and even enthusiasm have been manufactured by corporate propagandists and ideologues on a mission.

On the other side of this response to propaganda are the cynics who believe there is no point in being politically or civically engaged. There is nothing we can do about the state of the world. Consequently, it's better to cultivate our inner life and enjoy family and friends and forget about the polis. Such a reflexive cynicism not only feeds the core of corporate cultural domination, it reinforces political apathy.

Both responses encourage an anti-democratic political atmosphere. Both are ways of opting out of the democratic process. And, both leave a vacuum that the corporatists and power elite have no trouble filling.

It is with these ideas in mind that the authors of *Uncivil Liberties* have met, discussed, and collaborated on this collection of essays. We have learned much in the process of our collaborative efforts and have thoroughly enjoyed working as a team. Last year, four of us wrote a pamphlet, "Deconstructing Libertarianism," that is available on the Praxis website.[2] It was created quickly as a response to the film *Thrive*, which was enjoying widespread private screenings in the San Francisco Bay Area. Several non-profit organizations, including Praxis Peace Institute, were asked to show this film to their members. After reviewing the film and the *Thrive* website, we were alarmed by the anti-government, anti-community, narcissistic philosophy that emanated from this project.

We feel it is important to address the latest version of rightwing populism emanating from the airwaves, and we hope to contribute some antidotes for its venom. It is also important to contrast Civil Life with Uncivil Life and demonstrate the values that inform both modes of behavior. But, most of all, we feel the clock hand striking the fifty-sixth minute of the eleventh hour. In order to address the climate, financial, and poverty crises, we need to move from selfish behavior to a cooperative mode of relating.

Being willfully stuck in a rebellious stage of adolescent behavior—i.e., acting out, with external reality always self-referenced—will not solve any of these crises. Problems of such magnitude require maturity and cooperation. Through the ages, we have witnessed many examples of cooperation that saved a culture, tribe, or community. When people pull together and work together to achieve a goal, they are formidable. Labor unions, women's suffrage, the civil rights movement, and many other movements succeeded because people came together, collaborated on strategy, and helped each other along the way.

The times and crises we face today require vision, not the selfish and self-referenced behavior of a John Galt or his creator, Ayn Rand. When historian Arnold Toynbee identified the two factors that were present in civilizations that failed, he cited extreme concentrations of wealth and the failure to change when change was called for.

Economists wedded to obsolete ideologies are still touting various forms of predatory capitalism. They have no vision. And, without vision, as Proverbs warns, the people perish. Vision will come from the grassroots, not the halls of power. Vision cannot emerge from fear. It emanates from creative thinking, openness to new ideas, and the willingness to understand our limitations as well as our power.

Without historical background or context for the ideas floating around in the culture today, it is easy to fall prey to charged rhetoric and a logic that follows from false premises. This book is a small attempt to provide some context for the rhetoric. We examine the American myths that promote a "me first" agenda and the role that ideologies play in helping people make sense of their world. We look at specific libertarian proposals and deconstruct them piece-by-piece. We examine the experiment—still unproved—of American democracy. We cite successful alternatives to laissez-faire and corporate capitalism. These are alternatives that celebrate the dignity of humankind, that embody empathy, cooperation, respect, and love. It is with these qualities in mind that the six authors of this book have collaborated in a spirit of camaraderie and purpose. We hope it encourages dialogue, inquiry, and respectful discussion.

Georgia Kelly
Director, Praxis Peace Institute

NOTES

1   Marcuse, Herbert, *Eros and Civilization*, Boston: The Beacon Press, 1955, page 103.

2   www.praxispeace.org; www.praxispeace.org/pdf/DL_020612.pdf

CHAPTER ONE

THE MYTHIC FOUNDATIONS OF AMERICAN LIBERTARIANISM

By Barry Spector

*"Free money makes the rich strong and wise, while it corrupts poor people,
making them stupid and weak."*

—LEWIS LAPHAM

"You can be greedy and still feel good about yourself."

—IVAN BOESKY

"This is America. If you're not a winner, it's your own fault."

—JERRY FALWELL

TO UNDERSTAND WHY libertarianism (as opposed to anarchism[3])
has been popular in only one nation in the world—America—we need to
ground ourselves in mythological thinking.

The myth of American innocence is a story we have been telling
about ourselves for three hundred years. The idea of a nation divinely
ordained to save the world evolved so as to justify the original coloniza-
tion effort. Later, in changing conditions, it helped account for America's
unique and rapid expansion and its worldwide economic and cultural
domination.

It still moves us deeply because it inverts the guilt of history. It tells us that white colonizers were the actual victims of the westward expansion—attacked and massacred for no reason by evil savages emerging from the dark forests. Its subtext, of course, is our violent and racist history. But precisely because of this history, no nation has gone to such lengths to define itself by excluding so many from full membership *while regularly congratulating itself with pervasive stories of freedom and opportunity.* This is how we resolve the contradictions of our history and live with ourselves.

While white Americans across the entire political spectrum adhere to this myth in deep, often unconscious ways, libertarians exemplify it in its purest form. Their ideas of history, culture, and the relationship between the individual and the community reveal an essentially American, almost childlike innocence that borders on willful ignorance. Or, as the old joke goes, "Question: what's the difference between ignorance and apathy? Answer: I don't know and I don't care!"

First, let's get the easy issues out of the way.

1. We can quickly dismiss almost all politicians who claim to favor "small government" by examining their positions on military spending, foreign policy, domestic surveillance, corporate welfare, immigration, racial justice, gay marriage, medical marijuana, abortion, etc., all of which assume a large, centralized government and mandate state intervention in private lives.

    On the national scene, this leaves only Ron Paul, whose stated willingness to use the power of the federal government to outlaw abortion would seem to contradict his claim to be a libertarian. As for his anti-war views, activist Tim Wise writes, "Even a broken clock is right twice a day."[4]

2. Noam Chomsky disposes of the magical notion that American prosperity was built upon free markets: "Genocide and slavery: try to imagine a more severe market distortion than that."[5] We are talking about an entire hemisphere conquered

by military invasion and then distributed free to (very) select populations, who then went on to make their fortunes.

3. Americans are *already* taxed at far lower rates than other developed nations. This has meant miniscule social services and third-world levels of economic inequality. One cause of this situation is the tax code, which taxes ordinary income at up to 35 percent. The very rich, however, who receive most of their money from capital gains ("unearned income"[6]), pay only 15 percent. The situation was very different in the prosperous 1950s, when they were taxed at up to 90 percent.

As a mythologist, however, I am more interested in what we might call the mythic substrate of beliefs and attitudes that right-wing rhetoric engages so easily. Why are so many so willing to listen? Why, uniquely among nations, are we so stirred by hymns to freedom, riled up by rumors of government excess and enraged by the thought that one's hard-earned, raised-by-the-bootstrap money might be taxed for some vague sense of the "common good"?

AMERICAN MYTH

Our story describes a continent that was pure potential, the stuff of dreams. Since, in a European sense, the natives were not using the land productively, it was seen as "virgin" land, implicitly available for defloration and fertilization. Walter Raleigh made the analogy of land, woman, and rape very clear: Guiana "hath yet her maydenhead."

This is our creation myth of the American people, innocently arriving from diverse lands, charged with a holy mission to destroy evil, save souls, carve civilization out of the wilderness—and get rich. Professor R.W.B. Lewis wrote that this story saw the world: ". . . starting up again under fresh initiative, in a divinely granted second chance for the human race . . . [Americans were] emancipated from history, happily bereft of ancestry . . . Adam before the fall."[7]

The American dream-story was built up over four centuries of preaching, oratory, fiction, poetry, storytelling, popular songs, textbooks, advertisements, films, and television. Its essence was that *anything was possible.*

In this land of opportunity, one's greatness was limited only by his own desires. Americans like to believe in the *tabula rasa,* the "clean slate." Even now, we happily consume TV commercials for the military that encourage us to "be all you can be." The cliché moves us because it rests upon the old notion of human purpose. Americans, however, are constantly told that we can be anything we *want* to be. This is an adolescent misreading of the indigenous teaching that each person is born to be one thing only, and that the human challenge is to discover what it is.

By the late eighteenth century, Americans had developed a curious and contradictory mix of traditional Puritanism and modern Enlightenment values. Individuals were fallen and sinful, yet one could make of oneself whatever one might want. Indeed, in 1776—for the first time in history— a nation proclaimed the "pursuit of happiness" as its primary reason for existence.

America redefined the word liberty. On the one hand, liberty (from the Latin *liber,* an epithet of Dionysus, the Greek god of wine and madness) implies release, pointing toward *liberation,* in both its Marxist and Buddhist meanings. Liberty, however, has a continuum of meanings, including *permission* to do what one wants, the *power* to do what one likes, and the *privilege* to "take liberties" with others. Clearly, the passionate pursuit of liberty by some results in the destruction of the rights of others. In practical terms, freedom outside of an ethical framework—freedom without responsibility—becomes *license,* and it is inseparable from simple criminality. It is also inseparable from unfettered capitalism.

Early white Americans experienced a heady mix of the Puritan emphasis on personal salvation and the opportunistic disdain for class distinctions. For three centuries, free land in the west served as a safety valve for the discontented; thus, abject poverty was relatively uncommon. Most whites (prior to the mass immigrations of the late nineteenth century), to an extent unimaginable in Europe, became landowners.

But when extremes of wealth and poverty appeared, the rich felt little obligation to the poor. After all, declared Puritanism, *poverty was proof of sin.* Its belief in predestination survived as a Social Darwinism that has eviscerated the welfare state. And this thinking clearly underlies most libertarian pronouncements. When the poor are concerned, the idea of the *tabula rasa* recedes into the background.

To be a white American was to have the right to "make something of oneself." If one failed, he had no one to blame but himself. America, in our myth, became a nation of purposeless "self-made men," each individually making his destiny.

But curiously, the nation itself had a unique purpose. The myth proclaimed that God had chosen this people to spread freedom and opportunity. Eventually, Americans extrapolated this idea onto world affairs. *The nation of individualists became an individual among nations,* shaping other societies to its image of the good life. All empires have rationalized conquest, but only Americans justified enslavement and genocide with myths of freedom, good intentions, and manifest destiny. The Bush II administration carried this magical notion to its extreme, but it has always been the core of American policy.

The myth predicted inevitable progress toward the best of all possible worlds. Thus, *mobility* became a major value and history moved from east to west, allowing one to forget its lessons and continually exist in a "new" America. The ideal American was always moving toward something better, and he tended to look condescendingly upon those who held to the values of place. For the upwardly mobile, said James Hillman, to *be* is to be *stuck.*

The psychological implications are significant. Fifteen to twenty generations of restless Americans have come of age assuming that maturity implies freedom from all restraints, that family and community (and, for many men, all binding relationships) are to be *escaped from.* Historian James Robertson writes, "The ritual American act of courage is the declaration of independence-rebellion-migration of the American adolescent."[8]

Mobility evokes one of our most enduring themes: the *New Start.*

Always, one could pull up stakes, move on, start a new church, change one's name, and start over. Mobility also implies expansion: geographic, economic, and spiritual. Americans from the start have taken for granted the imperative to constantly expand and grow. This leads to wildly divergent yet surprisingly similar ideals—both the infinitely expanding consumer economy and "personal growth." New Age spirituality could not be more American.[9]

A mere half-century after the revolution, Alexis De Tocqueville observed of American preachers, ". . . it is often difficult to be sure when listening to them whether the main object of religion is to procure eternal felicity in the next world or prosperity in this."[10]

Eventually, religion and business merged as they did nowhere else. Without a state religion and with Protestant churches constantly splitting in schisms, each individual preacher was forced to become an entrepreneur of souls, a salesman, in order to distinguish his church from other churches. Consequently, a business-growth mentality grew within American Protestantism, and its philosophy of optimistic self-improvement merged with the capitalist ideology of greed and perpetual growth.

"New Start" also implies another old idea. In the tribal world, initiation removes youths from their community before returning them with their sense of purpose revitalized. It is *a point in time rooted within space.* But America inverted this ancient truth; since one could simply leave his community to acquire a new identity, initiation became *a point in space rooted in time.* As early as 1600, America symbolized the New Start for the entire western world. This aspect of the myth remains nearly as strong today. And it tells us that we rise up not as members of an ethnic group or social class, but as individuals.

THE MYTH OF INDIVIDUALISM

In an odd reversal of initiation motifs, the American heroic son "kills" his father symbolically—if he has one—by individuating, moving away, and repudiating everything the father stands for. In truth, we perceive family as at best a necessary evil, something to leave, so that one may get on with the pursuit of happiness. Progress happens through separation.

In terms of child-raising, Americans generally consider infants to be so fused with their mothers that we make every effort to encourage autonomy as early as possible. We hold and carry babies less than most nations do, admonishing them very early to be "big boys." The Japanese, by contrast, consider the infant to be utterly alien, as if from some strange, other world. Like most traditional people, they make every effort to enfold it within community as early as possible. Neither view of the child is right or wrong, says Hillman; both are myths, because they are "lived unconsciously, collectively as truths, performed unwaveringly as rituals."[11]

In the story of modernity, which is essentially an American story and unlike anything that came before, we have convinced ourselves that purpose can be divorced from community. But in a culture of consumerism, the desire to be seen as special produces a quest for expensive symbols—a quest that is ultimately futile, writes sociologist Phillip Slater, ". . . since it is individualism itself that produces uniformity."[12] Paradoxically, our American obsession with individualism produces persons who "cannot recognize the nature of their distress." This results in a desire to relinquish responsibility for control and decision-making to the images provided by the media. Here lies a great paradox of American life: our emphasis on the needs of the individual always constellates its shadow of cultural and political conformism.

But conformism and rebellious individualism are not our only choices. In the indigenous world, community exists in order to identify and nurture the *individuality* of each of its members, who are, in turn, necessary for the community to thrive and reproduce its values. Malidoma Somé writes that in West Africa, "Individuality is synonymous with uniqueness. This means that a person and his or her unique gifts are irreplaceable . . . A healthy community not only supports diversity, it requires diversity."[13]

Americans, when not involved in periodic moral crusades, valued the individual over the community more than any society in history. The opportunist argued for individual responsibility against the suffocating presence of big government. Determined on success, he was in a perpetual state of rebellion against authority (while ignoring the cavalry that protected his property, massive subsidies to the railroads, and later, a military-industrial complex that ensured his oil supply and markets for his products).

His wealth was proof that he lived in God's grace—and his neighbor's poverty indicated the opposite. But there was a price, writes Historian Greil Marcus: "To be an American is to feel the promise as a birthright, and to feel alone and haunted when the promise fails. No failure in America, whether of love or money, is ever simple; it is always a kind of betrayal."[14]

Whether in the relentless drive for wealth or in his obsession to know God's plan, the American, like no one before him, strove for self-improvement. Inside the word "improve," however, is the anxiety of one who can never positively know if he is saved. Thus he must continually "prove" his worth. He does so, he believes, only on his own merits. And he proves this worth only in relation to those who have less, those who (according to Puritanism) *deserve* less.

Mythmakers continually emphasize the individual over the collective. Most notably, Horatio Alger's nineteenth century dime-novel melodramas affirmed the Protestant virtues of frugality, hard work, and delayed gratification. His young heroes "pulled themselves up by their own bootstraps." These immensely popular stories of personal success counteracted populist agitation in a time when socialist ideas from Europe were questioning the mythic narrative.

AMERICAN DUALITIES

All societies confront the perennial conflict between individual and community. America's emphasis on individualism and its puritanical shadow produced a bewildering series of dualities that express, temporarily resolve, and often cover up this tension.

Early white fear and hatred of the dangerous, Indian *Other* created mythic opposites: the hero and the captive. Both our history and our psychology waver between the viewpoints of the helpless, innocent victim of pure evil, and the redeemer/hunter/hero, who vanquishes it and saves innocent Eden. By 1700, America's first coherent myth-literature appeared: potent tales of women who'd survived capture by the Indians.

The heroes of the western expansion became the stock characters of the second theme in American myth. The greatest, Daniel Boone, moved further west as civilization encroached, complaining, "I had not been two years at the licks before a d—d Yankee came, and settled down within an hundred miles of me!"

Whether Boone actually said that is irrelevant; Americans *needed* him to. The myth of the frontier contrasted Apollonian Cities with the Dionysian Wilderness (hence, three hundred years later, the spatial center of libertarianism in our Western states). The frontier was a safety valve of free western land when urban conditions became unmanageable, linking militarism with civilization's moral progress. Since society must grow or perish, it insisted on the racial basis of class difference and taught that such progress required the subjugation or extermination of both wild nature and savage races.

These themes had deep resonance, because they superficially resembled ancient hero myths. Both the hunter (willingly) and the captive (unwillingly) entered a primal world. If they could maintain their racial/cultural integrity there, they might incorporate its power, defeat its demons, and return to morally renew their community. It was initiation—and redemption—through violence.

The opposition of Puritan obsessions and the opportunists' predatory mania led to a division in the psyche that remains with us today. We regularly confront the opposing values of freedom and equality, framed as individualism versus conformism. To modern Puritans, all are equally sinful, requiring eternal vigilance to prevent infection. But descendants of the opportunists, from robber barons to anti-tax crusaders and sexual hedonists, venerate the sacred right to ignore community standards.

Conservatives (more appropriately: *reactionaries*) often intertwine these values, because one of the privileges of whiteness is to pick and choose among seemingly contradictory positions. Hence, we have the curious phenomena of gay Republicans who overlook their party's hatred of homosexuality; proponents of increased police presence who oppose gun control; others who oppose abortion rights but support capital punishment; and demagogues like Richard Nixon, who terrorized Middle America with warnings of *both* "the forces of totalitarianism and anarchy . . ."[15]

The pendulum has swung back and forth. Wherever one of these values predominates, its shadow soon constellates. The conflict emerges in the tension between libertarian hedonism and wartime conformism—often in the voices of the same persons. Another example is equal opportunity versus the meritocratic values of our institutions, and the old-boy networks that actually ensure continued WASP dominance.[16]

The consensus on the issue of equality is that all Americans have equal access to jobs, education, and housing. Assuming that all start on a "level playing field," we proclaim, "*May the best man win.*" The winners are those who "try hardest," applying the Protestant values of discipline and delayed gratification. Theologically speaking, they show by their success that they are among the elect of God.

Conflicts in the myth can emerge in terms of fairness versus cheating. The notion of fairness promises that all who play by the rules will prosper. Cheating breaks the rules but reveals our core, capitalist, individualist values. This explains our moral indignation about steroid abuse and rule violation in sports. Eldridge Cleaver saw that when all secretly subscribe to . . ."every man for himself," we see the weak as the prey of the strong. "But since this dark principle violates our democratic ideals," he wrote, ". . . we force it underground . . . sports are geared to disguise, while affording expression to, the acting out in elaborate pageantry of the myth of the fittest in the process of surviving."[17]

This story is myth not necessarily because it is untrue, but because its pervasiveness and its unexamined assumptions produce a consensus reality. It is a container of multiple and inconsistent meanings; its very ambiguity gives it the energy that motivates us.

It allows the privileged to select either one of the two polar ideals to justify themselves. For example, segregation—"separate but equal"—was legal for sixty years. Libertarians invoke equality to reject affirmative action, calling it reverse discrimination. Assistance to minorities only encourages laziness (the worst sin in Puritan theology). Though the argument is false, it has potency because it contains some truth: since individuals have occasionally succeeded on their own, then everyone should be able to. If others cannot, then it is their own fault.

Conservatives attack progressive legislation by invoking individualism, terrorizing working-class white males with the prospect of lost jobs and, paradoxically, suburban homogeneity. "Freedom" reverts to the right to accumulate and invest wealth without government regulation.

Marketing exploits both sides. As early as the 1830s, De Tocqueville noticed the tendency toward conformity that resulted from an ideology of equality in a materialistic society. Now, we purchase identical sunglasses, cigarettes, leather jackets, and motorcycles because *they symbolize rebellion against conformity*. Fashion is a simultaneous declaration of freedom and membership: we present a unique self to the world while looking like selected *Others*. "Individualists" often look and think, for the most part, within narrow parameters.

Military recruiters offer romantic images of individualistic warriors while simultaneously emphasizing the joys of dissolving oneself into the group. They seduce young men with images of noble knights in heroic, solo combat, conquering dragons in video games so as to entrain them in the automatic responses of large, anonymous armies.

Each contains the seed of its shadow. The conservative ideal of shrinking government inevitably produces restrictions on personal freedom and a prison-industrial complex.

Here is the essence of our story: both the Puritan and the Opportunist perceived freedom in autonomy and material possessions rather than in social relatedness. Eventually, both figures became somewhat interchangeable, as history transformed the aesthetic, religious notion of predestination into Social Darwinism and the secular culture of consumerism.[18]

The grand product of this mix was the American: enthusiastic, confident, practical, optimistic, extroverted, competitive, and classless. But to those who endured his excesses, he was arrogant, childish, narcissistic, and belligerent, the "Ugly American," innocently trampling tradition, making fine distinctions between the elect and the damned, or crushing the weak with astonishing cruelty.

Generally, a unique if superficial balance has ruled; the land of freedom and equality remains profoundly attractive to the world. Philosopher Jacob Needleman suggests the American ideal poses the ancient question of "what man is as opposed to what he can become."[19]

And yet, we have a Bill of Rights but no Bill of Responsibilities. Radicals find the source of the paradox of freedom and equality in unexamined definitions of just who is a member of the community, the *polis*. When only a small percentage of the population is admitted to that rarified atmosphere and all *Others* are excluded, then both the contradiction in the rhetoric and the sense of denial and innocence are heightened.

During wartime, we quickly forget the civil liberties that the nation was founded upon. Terrorized by the *Other*, we almost unanimously ignore or condone the grossest violations of the right to dissent.[20] This is Tocqueville's tyranny of the majority. For all their emphasis on individual rights, Americans have put so much emphasis on equality rather than upon diversity that they became intolerant of the very freedom to be different. He wrote, "I know of no country in which there is so little independence of mind and real freedom of discussion as in America."[21]

Over time, unrestrained capitalism provokes responses such as the New Deal. Franklin Roosevelt reframed freedom: of speech, of religion, from want and from fear. But after FDR's death, Harry Truman dropped the last two, replacing them with *freedom of enterprise*.

More fundamental to the American myth than ideals of freedom or equality, the unrestrained quest for wealth trumps them both. And yet, as noted above, during the Eisenhower administration, the rich paid extremely high income taxes, because (until the Reagan years) the consensus of social compassion still existed. Still, even now, corporate welfare, federal subsidies, and regressive taxation prop up big business and big agriculture; both would be horrified at the notion of a truly free market.

Yet the myth retains its pervasiveness, as middle class resistance to increased taxation on the super-wealthy indicates. Americans characteristically dream of becoming wealthy. Our sacred expectation of social mobility—the opportunity to move up into a higher social class—has been decreasing significantly for many years. But in a 2003 poll on the Bush tax plan, 56 percent of the *blue-collar* men who correctly perceived it as favoring the rich *still supported it.* The myth of the self-made man is so deeply ingrained in our national psyche that our ignorance of the facts is equaled only by our optimism: in 2000, 19 percent of respondents believed that they would "soon" be in the top one percent income bracket, and *another* 19 percent thought that they already were.

THE AMERICAN HERO

Myth is conveyed—and consumed—in narratives and images. So it is important to understand our most fundamental mythic image. The American obsession with individualism has been built up and buttressed by three centuries of stories, repeated in thousands of variations, of the lone hero.

Consider John Wayne in *Sands of Iwo Jima, Red River, The Searchers, She Wore A Yellow Ribbon,* and *The Horse Soldiers.* His characters and dozens of other film, TV, and comic book heroes are widowed, divorced, or uninvolved loners. They symbolize the man who has failed—or never attempted—the initiatory confrontation with the feminine depths of his soul. He carries with him the myth of violent redemption.

He does not strike first because, above all, he embodies the Puritan quality of self-control, which proves his superior character. And since his adversaries lack self-control, they embody the Dionysian *Other.* Not knowing his own darkness, he cannot symbolize genuine renewal.

All societies evolved versions of Joseph Campbell's classic "monomyth"—except America. The American hero is individualistic, lonely, extraordinarily powerful, selfless, and, like the Christ he is modeled upon, almost totally sexless.

Whereas the classic hero is born in community, hears a call, ventures forth on his journey and returns sadder but wiser, the American hero comes from elsewhere, entering the community only to defend it from malevolent attacks. He is without flaw but also without depth. He is *not* re-integrated into society.

Classic heroes often wed beautiful maidens and produce many children. But the American hero (with few exceptions such as comic anti-heroes) doesn't get—or even want—the girl. Wayne (in almost all of his roles), Hawkeye, the Virginian, Superman, Green Lantern, Spiderman, Rambo, Sam Spade, Indiana Jones, Robert Langdon, John Shaft, Captains Kirk, America, and Marvel: *all are single.* Their sexual aloofness ensures moral infallibility but also denies both complexity and the possibility of healing. In this mythology, women are merely excuses for the hero's quest.

The classic hero endures the initiatory torments in order to suffer into knowledge and renew the world. In this pagan and tragic vision, something always dies for new life to grow. But the American hero cares only to redeem ("buy back") others. Born in monotheism, he saves Eden by combining elements of the sacrificial Christ who dies for the world and his zealous, omnipotent father. The community begins and ends in innocence. And the Hero—*absolutely unique in all the world's mythologies*—remains outside of that community.

Only in our salvation-obsessed culture and in our movies does he appear. Then, he changes the lives of others without transforming them. This redemption hero has inherited an immensely long process of abstraction, alienation, and splitting of the western psyche. He exemplifies that peculiar process upon which our civilization rests: *dissociation.* He is disconnected from the *Other* (psychologically, his own unacknowledged darkness), whom he has demonized into his mirror opposite, the irredeemably evil. Since he never laments the furious violence employed in destroying such evil, he reinforces our characteristic American denial of death.

His appeal lies deep below rational thinking. He requires no nurturance, doesn't grow in wisdom, creates nothing, and teaches only violent resolution of disputes. This clearly has a modeling effect on millions of adolescent males in each new generation. Defending democracy through fascist means, he renounces citizenship. He offers vigilantism without lawlessness, sexual repression without resultant perversion, and moral infallibility without intellect.

Unlike the universal hero who lifts the veil between the worlds to discover eternal values, the redemption hero pulls the veil back down, confirms our innocence, and puts everyone back to sleep.

THE PARADOX OF THE OUTSIDER

The redemption hero, like Christ, leaves once his work is done. He must leave; he came from somewhere else, and he must return. However, as I have suggested, innocent Eden is defined by the existence of the *Other*—the external *Other* of terrorism, and internal *Other* of race. The *Other* is the outsider. Or: evil comes from outside, but so does redemption.

Riding off into the sunset, writes James Robertson, ". . . the cowboy hero never integrated himself with his society."[22] But he has quite a bit in common with his villainous adversary. Each rejects conventional authority, each despises democracy, and, although they serve opposing ends (like Ethan Edwards and Scar in *The Searchers*), their methods are similar.

The hero often becomes an outlaw (think *Rambo*) to defeat evil, because legitimate, democratic means are ineffective. Richard Slotkin writes that by the 1820s, the standard frontier hero of literature rescued captives by fighting the Indian "in his own manner, becoming in the process a reflection or a double of his dark opponent."[23] Eventually, the dual relationship in the mirror shatters and the villain must die, frequently in a *duel*. The one who can control himself defeats the one who cannot. In mythic terms, Apollo defeats Dionysus.[24]

Yet because he takes whatever he wants, has no responsibilities, and transgresses all moral codes, the villain is exciting and frankly attractive.

Americans admire outlaws. Newspapers described an 1872 hold-up by Jesse James as "so diabolically daring and so utterly in contempt of fear that we are bound to admire it and revere its perpetrators."[25] Fifty years later, when Al Capone took his seat at ballparks, people applauded. *The Godfather* is a regular candidate for the Great American Novel. In the era of capitalism's greatest profits, millions identified with the criminal families depicted in *The Sopranos* and *Growing Up Gotti*.

The policeman and the criminal express contradictory impulses within American character. Puritan zeal for order clashes with its equal, the frenzied quest for wealth. Critic Robert Warshow writes that the gangster is "what we want to be and what we are afraid we may become."[26] Both share still another characteristic: the villain's rage is a natural component of his pleasure in violating all boundaries, while the hero is also full of rage. Only by killing the villain, writes sociologist James Gibson, can he "release the rage accumulated from a life of emotional self-denial."[27]

Though the hero rejects society's rules, he is hardly alone; the desperado and the hedge fund CEO, whom we can't resist admiring, join him, along with all the *Others* who have been pushed beyond the walls or down into the underworld (a term which was first used to describe organized crime in the 1920s). Unlike in other countries, crime, organized or not, is a natural by-product of our value system, an alternative means of social mobility when "anything goes" in the pursuit of the symbols of success.

Again, we must note that, as Lapham argues, "...material objects serve as testimonials to the desired states of immateriality—not what the money buys but what the money says about our . . . standing in the company of the saved."[28]

When our assumptions of social mobility are revealed as fiction, however, the hero encounters his opposite—the victim—within himself, and we become (except perhaps for Nazi Germany) the most violent people in history.

These are the logical extremes to which libertarianism—either anarchy or a police state—would invite us, and the American psyche is too willing to follow.

THE RACE CARD

Exploring further into American myth, we inevitably confront the deeply racist nature of our society. American innocence is built upon fear of the *Other*—Indians, Mexicans, Asians, Communists, and terrorists, but always and primarily, African-Americans. The fact that, in our time, politicians and pundits regularly admonish progressives for playing the "race card" indicates the terrifying truth that the subject is taboo. And anthropology teaches us that what is taboo is *sacred*. Like the Hebrew god Jehovah, it is too holy to be named.

I contend that race (as fear, as white privilege, and as the underpinning of our entire economy) is the great unspoken—and therefore sacred— basis of our very identity as Americans.

White Americans know who they are because they are not the *Other*. In a culture built upon repression of the instincts, delayed gratification and a severe mind/body split, we have, for three centuries, defined the *Other* as those who cannot or will not restrain their impulses. And we continue to project those qualities upon Black people.

In this American context, the fear of government intrusion upon the individual too often serves as a euphemism for the concern that one's personally hard-earned assets (despite a legacy of white privilege) might be taken away and given to people who are too lazy to work for themselves.

These attitudes are essentially religious, even if articulated in secular terms. Underneath the clichés lies our still-powerful Puritan contempt for the poor. Surveys show that the majority of Americans deeply believe that losers are bad and morally corrupt. To fail economically is not simple failure but—in America—*moral* failure. And American myth does not distinguish between race and class.

Thus, the libertarian has a deeply religious argument for keeping all of his money. He rationalizes his greed with a secularized argument that subsidizing the poor will only encourage them in their laziness.

These themes have been played out with increasing effect since the end of the 1960s, when conservatives, far more literate in American myth than liberals, began to masquerade as rebels against the establishment. Their narrative took full advantage of the fact that American myth offers only one alternative to the hero—the victim. It emphasized "values" over "interests," redefining class war, again, in racial and cultural rather than economic terms. Although this fable was aimed at traditional, conservative men, undoubtedly many libertarians soaked up their own rhetoric, perceiving themselves as victims of greedy, inefficient, inappropriately compassionate bureaucrats.

Ronald Reagan's genius was to articulate hate within the wider myth of American inclusiveness, appealing to white males by evoking both ends of the mythic spectrum. He told them, writes Robert Bellah, that they could have it both ways: "You can . . . get rich, and you can also have the traditional values . . . have everything and not pay any price for it . . ."[29] They could be both Puritans and Opportunists. Reagan's backlash against the perceived excesses of the 1960s absolved whites of responsibility and renewed their sense of innocence and privilege.

Middle America supported leaders whose policies wrecked both the affluence and the family values that they held so dear. Indeed, Reagan managed the greatest shift of wealth in history, turning the world's most affluent nation into its greatest debtor nation.

He presided over a time during which, in a thousand subtle ways, government announced that the 300-year-old American social contract, the balance between freedom (the rights of the individual) and equality (the community's needs) was broken. The theme of his revolution was a return to small town values. But its subtext was greed, racism, contempt for the poor, and narcissistic individualism. Reagan gave white men permission to circle the wagons, retreat within the pale (pale skin), and reduce the *polis* to a size that excluded most of its inhabitants. To the ancient Athenians, someone who wouldn't participate in the welfare of the *polis* was an *idiota*. Reagan gave Americans permission to be idiots.

Ironically, one could trace the recent roots of this socially libertarian yet fiscally conservative fashion to the radical individualism of the sixties. Fritz Perls, a founder of the Human Potential Movement, had coined the ubiquitous statement of detachment from the *polis* seen on every t-shirt in those days: "I do my thing, and you do your thing. I am not in this world to live up to your expectations . . . you are not in this world to live up to mine . . . if by chance we find each other, it's beautiful. If not, it can't be helped."

Indeed, the U.S. Libertarian Party ran its first presidential candidate in 1972, just as the reaction against the 1960s was gaining steam.

White males, oblivious to their privilege, identified as victims—not of the rich, but of the minorities who were competing with them, the women claiming equality with them, the gays who publicly questioned the value of their masculinity, and the intellectuals who appeared to be telling them how to live. The conservative media barrage took advantage of the old tradition of anti-intellectualism. "Elite" now meant stuffy, superior, arrogant liberals who trivialized the concerns of ordinary people. The investment paid off; by 2000, only a fifth of Americans would describe themselves as liberal.

One of the primary objectives of the corporate media and our other mythic instructors is to distract Americans from identifying both the true spiritual and economic sources of their pain, and the actual opportunities for addressing them. Therefore, *the victim who cannot be a hero will search for villains or scapegoats.*

This is one way to understand right-wing activism: deeply committed, emotionally intense, sustained effort under the identification as victim, their targets being precisely those categories (race and gender) whom they have been educated to perceive as questioning or contesting that privilege.

Hence, we have, and certainly not for the first time in our history, groups of relatively well-off people who actually perceive themselves to be the victims of people who have far less than they do. And not just the relatively well-off. For example, I used to know a 50-year-old man who did odd jobs for me. He lived with his mother and was usually broke. Once, he declared that things were going badly for *middle-class people like him and me.* Middle-class? He was a good man, but the only way he could identify as middle-class was to remain blind to his own white privilege (and the welfare he was receiving).

This is the broader context behind Libertarianism. For at least the last twenty years, millions of Americans have described themselves as "liberal on social issues but fiscally responsible." Factoring out the complex issues of tax policy, jobs, crime, and the military, this translates as increasingly broad support for abortion rights, gay marriage, environmental protection, and de-criminalization of drugs on the one hand; and lower taxes on the other. With most Americans wanting to have their cake (freedom plus government services) without having to pay for it, it hardly seems surprising that a minority would be attracted to Libertarianism, which is, after all, merely an extreme expression of that which makes us all—exceptionally—Americans.

CODA: THE MYTH OF GROWTH

The goal of *Survivor,* television's most influential recent series, is to manipulate and scheme against other participants until only one winner is left. This perfectly exemplifies the American dogma of unlimited economic growth, which teaches that all must be free to achieve their potential through independent, meritorious (and if not, then creatively dishonest) action. Its relentless logic, however, turns nature into a resource and humans into only individuals rather than social animals. All motivation becomes self-interest, and no winners exist without losers.

Simplistic faith in "the market" mirrors fundamentalist faith in scriptural authority. In this story, the greatest sins are not violence but personal laziness (the crime of the Puritan) and social intrusion (the nightmare of the Opportunist). Government, by taxing successful individuals to sustain the needy, *calls this faith into question:* if everyone, even the poor, is entitled to basic human rights, then no one is automatically among the elect.

But we are talking about a belief system. The individual should be free to build, buy or waste whatever he wants. Then, the "rising boat" of generalized wealth may lift the less deserving along with it. Capitalism, argued J.M. Keynes, is the extraordinary belief that the nastiest of men, for the nastiest of reasons, will somehow work for everyone's benefit. When the freedom to grow trumps responsibility to the *polis*, however, "productivity" becomes a euphemism for "increased unemployment."

Long before recent Supreme Court decisions, the myth of growth enshrined the idea that abstract concepts devoted solely to accumulating capital—corporations—have all the rights of persons, plus limited liability and the freedom to externalize costs. Who are the gods of this theology? Corporations are immortal. They can reside in many places simultaneously, transform themselves at will, and do virtually whatever they choose, but they can't be imprisoned.

Corporate headquarters, like medieval religious shrines, are housed in America's tallest buildings. Americans express our aspiration to greatness through the metaphors of size, speed, height, expansion, acceleration, and constant action. Both territorial expansion and cultural influence have been our manifest destinies. We outrun the competition and climb out of ignorance up the rungs of the ladder of evolution. Great music "uplifts" us. The Greater grows by "rising" out of the lesser. Consider some books on American history: *The Rise of American Civilization, The Rise of the Common Man,* and *The Rise of the City.* Both intoxication and euphoria are "highs." Depressive individuals are "down" and bad news is a "downer."

Counter-arguments produce anxiety, because we perceive them as attacks upon the faith itself. If one grows from wet/dark/feminine to dry/light/masculine, then appeals to sustainability become entwined with threats to masculinity. Male identity converges with the imperative to grow; everything is bound up in "potential" and "potency." Bigger is not simply better, but the only alternative to "smaller," as "hero" is to "loser." Jimmy Carter suggested mild limits to growth and was destroyed politically for the attempt. Studying his fate, Reagan, Clinton, both Bushes, and now Obama have praised limits to government, despite increasing its size.

The belief that the imperative of growth trumps life itself underlies all corporate and most government policies. Conservatives attack big government, but praise its responsibility to support the private sector through subsidies, infrastructure, and military intervention—all forms of

externalizing costs. The result is an economy, writes Hillman, that is ". . .
the God we nourish with actual human blood."[30]

The holy text of this myth, the *Gross Domestic Product*, symbolizes the
pathology of growth in four ways. First, it counts all economic activity as
valuable, such as the $20 billion we annually spend on divorce lawyers, and
never distinguishes between textbooks and porn magazines. It includes
every aspect of a death from lung cancer: medical, hospital, pharmaceuti-
cal, legal, and funereal, as well as growing, transporting, packaging, marketing, and disposal of tobacco products. Increased gas expenditures add
to the GDP without a corresponding subtraction for the toll fossil fuels
take on the thermostatic and buffering functions of the atmosphere. Luxury buying by the rich covers up a lack of necessary buying by the poor. So
the GDP actually disguises suffering. The ultimate example is war: exceptionally costly, energy-intensive, requiring lengthy cleanup. By adding to
the GDP, however, it builds an artificial sense of economic health.

Second, judging profitability on quarterly stock reports leads to maximizing short-term strategies (such as investing in the SUV rather than in
energy-efficient cars) at the cost of long-term losses.

Third, even if it were of any real value, the GDP is wildly inaccurate because
it ignores the massive underground economy of drugs and gambling.

Fourth, it doesn't count the real, natural economy. Robert F. Kennedy
said it "measures everything . . . except for that which makes life worth-
while." Most crucial life-supporting functions take place not through the
market, but through social processes and voluntary activities (families
and churches) or through completely natural processes (the cooling and
cleansing functions of trees, etc.). None register in the GDP until something destroys them and people have to buy substitutes in the market. In
this mad calculus, fuel conservation, stable marriages, and children who
exercise and eat healthy foods are *threats* to the economy.

Many "progressives" are also unaware of the pervasiveness of this story.
Clearly, recession hurts the poor most. But we reveal ignorance of our
myths when we demand larger shares of an ever-expanding economic
pie, or lament "underdevelopment" in other nations. Growth, whether

inequitable or sustainable, leads inevitably to the terrifying vision of seven billion people each driving their own SUV.

Eastern wisdom teaches that we can never satisfy the soul's hunger with material food alone. Yet self-improvement and growth are such bedrock American values that, by the 1970s, they were, once again, models for the spiritual life. Hillman argued that the first assumption of the "therapeutic culture" is that emotional maturity entails a progressive differentiation of self from others, especially family. *American psychology mirrors its economics: the heroic, isolated ego in a hostile world.*

For a significant segment of the population, "inner growth" replaced the old ideal of the democratic citizen. Well-meaning people, more American than they knew, spoke of what they could get from life, rather than, to paraphrase John Kennedy, what they could give to it. Spiritual growth became another version of the pursuit of happiness, now defined by "heightened awareness" and "peak" experiences. "Feeling good," wrote psychologist Lesley Hazleton, became "no longer simply a right, but a social and personal duty."[31] And the economy offered the material symbols that gave evidence—proof, in Puritan terms—of spiritual "growth."

This idea takes its energy from two older ones: life-long initiation and biological maturation. But it has split off from the natural and indigenous worlds in its unexamined assumptions. All living things die and return to Earth, but a "growing" person, by definition, cannot. Initiation requires the death of something that has grown past its prime. And worse, since the myth of growth (material or spiritual) is essentially a personal story, it narcissistically assumes the unlimited objectification and exploitation of others for the ultimate aggrandizement of the Self.

We find unlimited growth in neither nature nor culture, but only in the cancer cell, which multiplies until it destroys its host. The miracle of reproduction serves death instead of life. Growth inevitably evokes its opposite. The body produces *anti*bodies, which destroy the invasion of grandiosity. There is no more basic ecological rule. Natural growth only occurs within a broader cycle that also includes decay.

But when growth, potency, happiness, pressure to be in a good mood, to "have a nice day," to be "high" are hopelessly intertwined with con-sumer goodies, *not* having them means a drop into shame, depression, and victimization. In the real world of limited resources, growth is a Ponzi scheme in which our great-grandchildren subsidize our innocent and nar-cissistic fantasies.

NOTES

3   Noam Chomsky claims that in most parts of the world, the terms "libertar-ian" and "libertarianism" are synonymous with Left anarchism. "The Week Online Interviews Chomsky" (www.zcommunications.org/the-week-online-interviews-chomsky-by-noam-chomsky): "The term libertarian as used in the U.S. means something quite different from what it meant historically and still means in the rest of the world. Historically, the liber-tarian movement has been the anti-statist wing of the socialist movement. Socialist anarchism was libertarian socialism. In the U.S., which is a soci-ety much more dominated by business . . . it means eliminating or reduc-ing state controls, mainly controls over private tyrannies. Libertarians in the U.S. don't say let's get rid of corporations. It is a sort of ultra-rightism."

4   www.timwise.org/2012/01/of-broken-clocks-presidential-candidates-and-the-confusion-of-certain-white-liberals/#more-903

5   Chomsky, Noam. *Understanding Power—The Indispensable Chomsky.* Eds. Mitchel, Peter R. and John Schoeffel. New York: *The New Press, 2002,* p. 255–7. Indeed, almost all developed countries originally got rich not through free markets, but through tariff protection and military con-quest. Nineteenth and early twentieth century U.S. tariffs of 40 to 50 percent were the highest in the world. Later, the U.S. government paid for 50 to 70 percent of the country's total expenditures on research and development from the 1950s through the mid-1990s, usually under the cover of defense spending (Ha-Joon Chang, *Bad Samaritans: The Myth of Free Trade and the Secret History of Capitalism,* Bloomsbury, 2007).

6   Another definition of "unearned income" is *welfare.*

7   Lewis, R.W.B. *The American Adam. Chicago: University of Chicago Press, 1959,* p. 5.

8   Robertson, James O. *American Myth American Reality. New York: Hill & Wang, 1980,* p. 149–50.

9   Consider the massively popular book, *The Secret* (2006, 21 million copies in 44 languages), by Rhonda Byrne. In the film version, a series of self-help teachers promote positive thinking, primarily toward the goal of acquiring consumer goods and a great love life. This tradition extends back to the New Thought teachers of early nineteenth-century America. The film ignores the values of community almost totally.

10   De Tocqueville, Alexis. *Democracy in America*. Ed. Richard D. Hefner. New York: New American Library, 1955, p. 403.

11   Hillman, James. "Myths of the Family." (Audio Cassette, Sound Horizons Presents).

12   Slater, Phillip. *The Pursuit of Loneliness: American Culture at the Breaking Point*. Boston: Beacon Press, 1972, p. 20–30.

13   Somé, Malidoma. *The Healing Wisdom of Africa*. New York: Tarcher/Putnam, 2000, p. 91–92.

14   Marcus, Greil. *Mystery Train: Images of America In Rock 'n Roll Music*. New York: Plume/Penguin, 1997, p. 20.

15   Slotkin, Richard. *Gunfighter Nation: The Myth of the Frontier in 20th-Century America*. New York: Harper, 1992, p. 617.

16   The C-grade High School student George W. Bush was the ultimate "Legacy" admission at Yale.

17   Cleaver, Eldridge. *Soul On Ice*. New York: Ramparts Books, 1968, p. 84.

18   Spector, Barry. *Madness at the Gates of the City: The Myth of American Innocence*. Berkeley: Regent Press, 2010, Chapter Seven.

19   Needleman, Jacob. *The American Soul*. New York: Tarcher, 2002, p. 13, 145.

20   On September 10, 2001, G.W. Bush was the most unpopular president in our history. On the 12th, he had a 90 percent approval rating.

21   De Tocqueville, Alexis. *Democracy in America*. Ch. 15.

22   Robertson, James O. *American Myth American Reality*. New York: Hill & Wang, 1980, p. 164.

23   Slotkin, Richard. *Regeneration Through Violence: The Mythology of the American Frontier, 1600–1860*. Middletown, CT: Wesleyan University Press, 1973, p. 563.

24   The Greeks, however, knew better. In myth, the hyper-rational god Apollo willingly left his shrine at Delphi for three months every year so that his irrational, mad half-brother Dionysus could move in.

25   Quoted by Lapham, Lewis, in *Harper's Magazine*, September 2003, p. 9. This is a regular theme in cinema: in 1931 alone, Hollywood produced

over fifty gangster movies in which the bad guys get away without being punished.

26 Gitlin, Todd. *Media Unlimited: How the Torrent of Images and Sounds Overwhelms Our Lives.* New York: Holt, 2002, p. 201.

27 Gibson, James W. *Warrior Dreams: Violence and Manhood in Post-Vietnam America.* New York: Hill and Wang, 1994, p. 80.

28 *Harper's Magazine.* May 2003, p. 8.

29 Bellah, Robert. "Individualism and the Crisis of Civic Membership." *The Christian Century.* March 20, 1996.

30 Hollis, James. *Tracking the Gods: The Place of Myth in Modern Life, Studies In Jungian Psychology By Jungian Analysts.* Toronto: Inner City, 1995, p. 26.

CHAPTER TWO

THE INDIVIDUAL AND CIVIL SOCIETY

By Georgia Kelly

"Taxes, after all, are the dues that we pay for the privileges of membership in an organized society."

—FRANKLIN D. ROOSEVELT

AT LEAST SINCE the presidency of Ronald Reagan, the celebration of the isolated individual has triumphed in American culture. We honor the hero and laud the over-achiever. We romanticize winners, celebrities, and the rich and famous. Our culture promotes the myth that we too can have it all. Consequently, many Americans grow up with aspirations of fame and fortune. The fact that it is impossible for every American to become part of the "one percent" only seems to inflate the myth. We believe in our personal exceptionalism the same way our country believes in its national exceptionalism.

Today, many children have aspirations of becoming CEOs when they grow up, even though they have no idea what the job description means. The fact that their real goal is wealth, instead of a meaningful occupation, says volumes about our culture. They are not talking about becoming doctors, teachers, or social workers. By cultivating a fantasy world that promises the gold instead of focusing on creating a useful product or service, the individual is separated from community. Unrealistic or naïve aspirations might find faux fulfillment through voyeurism and projection. Reality TV, video games, and celebrity culture are only too willing to provide the projection screen.

Along the way, we have forgotten the other dimension of who we are. We are both individuals and members of society, and this complex relationship comes together in civil society, that network of rich voluntary relationships. Civil society cannot be understood only in terms of individuals; it also requires considering our relationships with one another and our individual capacity to enter into them due to supportive institutions, which includes government.

When individuals focus entirely on their own development and aspirations, unconnected from community, there will be a corresponding disconnect from political culture. Apathy and naiveté will bolster an ahistorical political sensibility. Their choices in the political arena will be seen as unique. Their candidate will be the most pure and like no other candidate before him or her unless it is to hark back to a nearly mythical American president who is long dead. They tend to embrace an ideology that will solve all problems while simultaneously denying issues that are too complex.

CRISIS IN EDUCATION

Many citizens in the United States are no longer taught the basics of government and their role in it. The lack of required civics classes in high school and a media that focuses on trivia and voyeurism instead of substantive issues that affect people's lives has led to widespread ignorance of how government works and the role that citizens can play in forming and transforming their government.

To cite a typical example, late-night television host Jay Leno interviewed a group of visitors to the nation's capitol in the "Jaywalking" segment of his show. Not one person he interviewed could name the number of senators representing their state in Washington. One teacher, with students standing nearby, proclaimed with confidence that his state sent "30 representatives" to the U.S. Senate![32]

Becoming aware of the general lack of knowledge and interest in governance are important steps in learning how and why many people are manipulated by buzz words, emotionally provocative slogans, and bravado that often masquerades profound ignorance.

The right-wing and libertarian attacks on all things government, including the defunding of education, have gone a long way toward dumbing down our educational system. Compared with European and many Asian countries, the U.S. is lagging behind. Defunded public education is not likely to provide this knowledge any time soon. It has become clear in recent years that citizens must take it upon themselves to become civically literate.

Commenting on the dire situation of education in America, *New York Times* columnist Paul Krugman warns of the cumulative consequences of defunding education:

> *Until now, the results of educational neglect have been gradual—a slow-motion erosion of America's relative position. But things are about to get much worse, as the economic crisis—its effects exacerbated by the penny-wise, pound-foolish behavior that passes for "fiscal responsibility" in Washington—deals a severe blow to education across the board.*[33]

GOVERNMENT IS ESSENTIAL TO CIVIL SOCIETY

In addition to education, the libertarian attack on government, at least since the Reagan era, has done great damage to many other areas of society. After all, it was the libertarian agenda pushed by Alan Greenspan and his Ayn Randian cohorts that encouraged bundled mortgage loans and derivatives that gambled away peoples' pensions, savings, and homes. Government regulations could have prevented the housing bubble and subsequent foreclosure debacle. At one time, we had such regulations, but that was before the right-wing demonization of government.

Another target for right-wing invective concerns taxes. Libertarians will tell you that taxes are theft. They assume that everything an individual accomplishes is done on his or her own. As Elizabeth Warren, creator of the Consumer Protection Agency and recently elected U.S. senator, so accurately noted:

> *There is nobody in this country who got rich on their own. Nobody.*
> *You built a factory out there—good for you. But I want to be clear.*
> *You moved your goods to market on roads the rest of us paid for. You*
> *hired workers the rest of us paid to educate. You were safe in your*
> *factory because of police forces and fire forces that the rest of us paid*
> *for. You didn't have to worry that marauding bands would come and*
> *seize everything at your factory.*[34]

To paraphrase Oliver Wendell Holmes, taxes are what we pay for civilized society. Public education; city and national parks; the roads, bridges, and public transportation that connect us; and the social systems that returns some of our tax money through Medicare, Social Security, and veteran benefits are all the result of taxes. These are benefits of a civilized society.

Investing in the commons, in the people, and in the future of our nation requires a commitment to the society in which one lives. Of course, this requires an educated and mature citizenry, not one stuck in a rebellious phase of development that focuses doggedly on individual rights with little or no regard for the individual's responsibility to civil society. Many libertarians do not consider that an educated and informed citizenry might actually create a government by, of, and for the people who pay the taxes.

One of the questions I had in preparing this book was: how can one inspire good citizenship? What would make knowledge of civic affairs sexy, the way football games, shopping, reality shows, or celebrity gossip are for many people? This is the challenge. When we have a media that distracts people with reality TV instead of informing them about the reality of issues that matter, we have a democracy problem. An unengaged, uninformed public turns its back on democracy, which creates a vacuum in the polis that is often filled by corporate lobbyists, power seekers, and others who do not have the public interest in mind.

LIBERTARIANS SEEKING POLITICAL POWER

There is a small but strong libertarian movement determined to dismember governmental agencies it dislikes and allow the "free" market to have its way in our country. This movement is influential far beyond its small numbers because it manipulates symbols and slogans strongly connected to our national self-image. Therefore, it is important to identify some of the most extreme forms of libertarian ideology and to project what the fallout would be if they were actually enacted.

The Film *Thrive*

The film *Thrive* and its accompanying website,[35] created by Procter & Gamble heir Foster Gamble, put forth a variety of libertarian fantasy proposals in mapping his ideal world. They include the following:

> ➤ *Limit government and government control. Result: no regulations to reign in corporations or to check greed; nothing to protect against global warming (Gamble is not convinced that global warming exists or if it does that it is caused by humans), toxic substances, untested drugs, and more.*
> ➤ *Roll back social programs, eliminate government subsidies, and severely limit or eliminate taxes. The results of enacting these ideas would mean no funding for Social Security, Medicare, public education, and possibly even police and fire departments.*
> ➤ *Thrive praises voluntary systems, but this confuses many meanings of the term.*
>> • Voluntary education. There would be no government requirements for education, and public education would be phased out. Gamble's idea, as with many libertarians,

is "to keep government out of education and allow people to choose the education they desire." The fact that some people would get little or no education is an inconvenient truth they choose to ignore.

- Create a private highway system of toll roads. Would each road owner have his or her own payment system? Private highways would appear to make a relatively simple system (that we enjoy today) ridiculously complicated.

- Dismantle the Justice Department and create private judicial systems that are private and competitive! Would more bribes reap lower fines and a "get out of jail free" card?

- Allow private armies. Imagine roving gangs of angry, armed white men serving warlords and corporations— and, who are not subject to civil control!

➤ *Establish a Truly "Free" Market. This is perhaps the most astonishing error in the film, Thrive. After experiencing the extreme free market strategies and near-elimination of regulations by libertarian Alan Greenspan, the Thrive website still maintains that we need not just fewer regulations, but NO regulations! Instead, they propose the "utopian" free market as envisioned by Ayn Rand. At the very least, they seem oblivious to the consequences of such ideas, even with history arguing against them at every turn.*

A quote from the *Thrive* website explains a basic tenet of libertarian ideology.

> *"We have never experienced a truly free market without government intervention. There would be tremendous innovation, diversity and growth to create thriving economic systems."*

It is a mystery of millennial proportions why innovation and growth would suddenly spring forth fully formed like Athena from the head of Zeus, simply because we have no government intervention. There is no prior example of such a success story—now or in the past—that would substantiate such a deluded theory. However, if we are seeking states without a central government—a presumed libertarian paradise from which to learn—we might consider Somalia.[36]

As Thom Hartmann writes about libertarianism,

> *They claim that their vision of a truly free world . . . had never been tried before on the planet. Their opponents said that indeed their system had been tried, over and over again throughout history, and in fact was itself the history of every civilization in the world during its most chaotic and feudal time.*[37]

The twentieth century has been a century of unequaled innovation and of the growth in responsibilities taken on by all democratic governments. The Internet, to give but one example, is a government contribution to American life.

The Ron Paul Phenomenon

What attracts many quasi liberals to Ron Paul is his opposition to the wars in Iraq and Afghanistan and his advocacy for legalizing marijuana. Auditing or abolishing the Federal Reserve is another position of his that garners considerable favor. Probing Paul's ideas often ends there. Because Paul says what he believes no matter how popular or unpopular the ideas, he has earned credibility for consistency and honesty. These are very attractive qualities in a political field noted for their absence. They are also very attractive qualities if one is seeking a political "savior" who rides in on the proverbial white horse to rescue us.

Ron Paul doesn't believe in a government healthcare option. He seems to believe that charity for the poor will suffice. But empathy doesn't appear to be high on the libertarian list of personal attributes, so what would charity mean in a libertarian world?

Paul believes that the Department of Education should be

abolished—not reformed, abolished! How does private and voluntary education lead to a society of literate people? Sure, the wealthy would profit from the best education that money could buy, but everyone else would be left to improvise. Thomas Jefferson emphasized that public education is a necessary step forward in empowering the people in a society. Democracy is not possible without an educated public. But that brings us to another American cornerstone that many libertarians reject, democracy itself. This rejection of democracy should be a red alert warning about their agenda.

Paul believes that Global Warming is "a hoax." In spite of all the evidence to the contrary and the near unanimous agreement among scientists, accepting the obvious is at odds with his ideology. Facts are not allowed to contradict the theory.

He opposes choice for women while insisting that he supports Civil Rights, though obviously not for women. But, he also opposes the Civil Rights Act of 1964. States rights flourished in the old South, but individual freedom did not fare so well. The inconsistencies are numerous, but rarely is Ron Paul called to account for them.

As Katha Pollitt wrote in *The Nation*, "Ron Paul has opposed almost every piece of progressive legislation that was passed in the last 200 years! He opposed Federal Deposit Insurance and continues to oppose Roe v. Wade. He would abolish the Environmental Protection Agency, governmental regulations on health and safety (OSHA), and the Federal Aviation Authority."[38] What would life be like if there were no environmental protection agency? If DDT and asbestos had not been banned? If unleaded gasoline had not been mandated and smog still blanketed most American cities? If standards for clean water were not in place? Might we have a cholera epidemic or other water borne diseases? These critical concerns are ignored by libertarians who think the market will determine our safety. We have seen how that worked before regulations were in place. The market almost always puts profit first, not safety.

Islands without Governments

Peter Thiel, co-founder of PayPal, has funded a "seasteading" foundation in hopes of launching a libertarian utopia. The plan is to create self-governing islands 200 miles off the California coast that can serve as experiments in libertarian political, social, and legal systems.[39] What comes to mind is a twenty-first century version of *Lord of the Flies*.

For those who really believe that such an island would foster anything but selfish behavior, its manifestation would be an interesting proving ground. I assume that most inhabitants of said island would be white and male and that women would never amount to more than one-third of their population, as there is a very low percentage of women attracted to libertarianism. That alone could create problems in paradise.

Perhaps this island would be somewhat like Las Vegas today, where money is all that ultimately matters. The rich are treated like kings and the poor are out of sight. Debtors' prisons might be another anachronistic innovation in case the islands' workers fell behind in rent payments.

The reactionary programs sold as a "vision" on the *Thrive* website, or in Peter Theil's future island experiment, or in Ron Paul's political prescriptions are nothing short of a dark fantasy that would catapult us back to the nineteenth century with "voluntary" types of social regulation, i.e., no taxes, no labor laws, no child labor laws, no environmental regulations, no Social Security, no Medicare, no public education, no civil rights, and no government programs of any kind. We see how well that worked out in the era of robber barons, slavery, and the unbridled exploitation of man and nature.

Libertarians tend to focus almost entirely on "liberty" while responsibility and civil society are rarely, if ever, mentioned. They also fail to address greed, the need to limit growth, or the individual's responsibility to society.

MORE QUESTIONS, MORE FANTASIES

Cults are famous for their refusal to be influenced by inconvenient facts. Libertarianism, in many ways, resembles a cult.

Libertarians claim that cutting taxes will create jobs, but have we seen any evidence? In the past several years, corporations have paid fewer, if any, taxes. Some corporations get refunds when they haven't paid taxes. For example, in 2010, Bank of America paid no taxes and received a $1.9 billion tax refund. Exxon Mobil's 2009 profits totaled $19 billion, and according to SEC filings, they received a $156 million rebate.[40] After their great rebate, did Bank of America hire more people? No, they cut 30,000 jobs.[41] Likewise, General Electric received a $4.1 billion tax refund but cut one-fifth of its American jobs.[42]

While corporate windfalls have increased salaries at the top, they have not created new jobs. In fact, corporations have been eliminating jobs through downsizing, automation, and outsourcing, which have resulted in gargantuan reward pay for CEOs and obscene compensation packages when they choose to move on or retire. Tax cuts have not created jobs, nor are they likely to do so any time soon.

Many libertarians buy organic food, protest the inclusion of GMOs (genetically modified organisms) in fruits and vegetables, and buy only free-range meats and poultry. Who do they think would regulate the industry if not a government that doesn't profit from said businesses? And how exactly would eliminating government regulations lead to reigned-in corporations? Without government intervention, corporations would be completely free to wreak havoc on the populace and the environment. Beijing, the most polluted city in the world, gives us a good twentieth century example of the absence of bothersome air quality standards. The non-violation idea put forth in the film *Thrive* and by many libertarians is a lovely concept, but history shows us that some people will always violate or exploit others when they are free to do so.

Freedom, libertarians never tire of telling us, generates inequality. But, they never tell us how inequality can destroy freedom. To safeguard

freedom we need to prevent the abuse of inequality. It is critical to acknowledge what fallout would ensue from a further deregulated "free" market.
An example of the laissez faire adage "let the market decide" can be seen
in the way employees at Walmart are treated. Among other things, the
anti-union behemoth pays low wages to its employees in the U.S. and supports near slave conditions in Bangladesh garment factories.[43] Recently,
Walmart had to pay more than $4.8 million in back pay and damages to
workers for overtime pay they did not receive. There have been at least
three previous settlements with the Department of Labor due to unpaid
overtime wages.[44]

Without regulation of any kind in this country, who or what would
stop wages from plummeting further or protect workers from exploitation and hazardous working conditions? Who or what would prevent
people from selling themselves into slavery if that would be the only way
to survive in a libertarian society? Some libertarian thinkers actually
argue that a person should be "free" to sell him or herself into slavery in
order to survive. It may be an alternative to debtors' prison in a libertarian paradise.

WHAT'S WRONG WITH MANY NEW AGE RESPONSES TO LIBERTARIANISM

As Barry Spector points out in this book, "new age spirituality could not
be more American." It too promotes endless growth, albeit of a spiritual
nature, but it still holds the belief that unlimited growth is desirable. Personal growth has no limits. Spiritual accomplishment is never ending.
Nirvana is always out of reach, so we must continue to "grow" in order to
get closer to it. The idea of limits has not been part of the American story,
so it is not surprising that the American interpretation of Eastern philosophy has been sculpted to fit our cultural bias. Non-attachment has often
been interpreted to mean that there is an elitist quality of being above and
not of the world. The quest for enlightenment became a competitive spiritual sport, which became known as "spiritual materialism." It is time to

realize how our cultural bias determines our frames of reference and the way we interpret the traditions of other societies. It's past time to update our story for the twenty-first century.

New age thinking is also aligned with the desire to find common ground, which can be a good thing. But, there is also a tendency to be critical of boundaries and discernment. The latter is often referred to as "judgment." When peace is desired above all else, denial is one way to bypass the stumbling blocks that require discernment. Maybe the lesson here is that a premature easy peace is no peace at all.

Another kind of new age fallout is the desire to please others or to find common ground to the point of conflict aversion. Taken to an extreme, avoiding conflict leads away from taking principled stands even when they are called for. Such weak responses to right-wing ideologies shut off critical thinking and accept their rant instead of challenging it. It is from this weakened state that one often enables destructive policies, all the while claiming innocence regarding the consequences of not standing up for principles. Choosing to focus only on areas of agreement is a form of denial. Avoiding conflict does not lead to peace; it's the responsible and respectful handling of differences that establishes peaceful principles.

WHAT'S WRONG WITH MANY QUASI-LIBERAL RESPONSES TO LIBERTARIANISM

When the public's distaste for unnecessary wars is a major factor in winning votes, Ron Paul might look attractive to people who do not examine his complete ideology. In order to break the spell of one-issue dominance, we must be able to articulate the many flaws in this ideology and identify reasons why it is so dangerous for the future of our country. Gus diZerega has thoroughly deconstructed these flaws and inconsistencies in this book. He demonstrates that libertarians do not understand their own principles and have never shown much interest in trying to use them as more than slogans for opposing "the state."

RECOGNIZING COMMON GROUND BETWEEN PROGRESSIVES AND LIBERTARIANS WHILE ACKNOWLEDGING OUR DIFFERENT WORLDVIEWS

It would be inadmissible to pass over the areas of common interest between progressives and libertarians. Though Ron Paul opposes choice for women, most libertarians have supported the right to choose. They also support gay marriage. Most also oppose capital punishment, unnecessary wars, and government wiretapping and surveillance of citizens, which would be in agreement with most progressives. We too would like an audit of the Federal Reserve.

In areas where we can work together, we should certainly do so because our combined efforts will help create the changes we hope to enact. But, what we must not lose sight of is the difference in our worldviews. Our analyses and perspectives come from different values and a different way of looking at the values we share. We start with different premises about the way the world works and what our role is in it, but respectful dialogue and debate is what democracy is all about and could make for interesting and educational discourse.

WHAT IS TO BE DONE? PROGRESSIVE SOLUTIONS

Civil society should be rich and multifaceted. It should enable any citizen to pursue his or her dreams and hopes, so long as doing so does not make it more difficult for others to do the same. Unlike libertarian fantasies, there are working models that thrive in today's world. There are also many examples of how government can serve a richer civil order.

The Mondragón Cooperatives

There are many examples of civil society created for the benefit of all. One of the most successful models is the Mondragón Cooperatives in the Basque region of Spain. Unlike libertarians, Mondragón's members have tested and realized their vision in real life, beginning nearly sixty years ago with one business and five worker-owners. Today, Mondragón includes 120 worker-owned businesses ranging from small businesses to major industries, and has nearly 100,000 worker-owners. The workplace is democratically managed, with hierarchy limited to management functions and the placement of people with specific skills. One of their core principles is "wage solidarity," with CEOs' salaries at six times the workers' lowest pay. In the four seminars that Praxis has organized at the Mondragón Cooperatives, we learned that Mondragón always puts "people before profit." This is in keeping with another of their core principles, *"the instrumental and subordinated nature of capital."*

Does this mean that Mondragón lags behind businesses and corporations that support a "free" market ideology? Quite the contrary. Mondragón has its own bank, Caja Laboral, with more than 380 branches located throughout Spain. A bank which, as of early 2012, was still lending in spite of the economic woes in Spain today. Mondragón supports its own social services, pensions, and healthcare, and boasts the largest research and development center in Europe with fourteen separate entities. There is zero unemployment in the Mondragón businesses, while Spain's overall unemployment hovers around 25 percent (as of December 2012).

The American myth says we can "have it all." But compared with Mondragón's view, that seems provincially (or arrogantly) naïve. Why should we even want "it all"? The countries and communities that value social connection, social services, and the eradication of poverty consistently appear at the top of the happiness index and are in fact generally quite prosperous. Sixty years ago, the Basque region was the poorest area of Spain. Today, the Basque region has the highest standard of living and the lowest unemployment rate in Spain. What accounts for this transformation? One reason is that it has the largest number of people involved in worker-owned businesses and the largest number of people working cooperatively. The Basque region avoids the extremes. There are neither mansions on the hill nor poverty in the streets. The town of Mondragón is solidly middle class and comfortable for everyone.

Mondragón is one example of a proven model that works along cooperative and social lines. It does not praise individual egoism, but rather focuses each person within a social context that honors and respects both the individual and the community. The Mondragón Cooperatives, like many other successful worker-owned organizations worldwide, have been built from a holistic vision grounded in a practical sensibility.

Often, when I have cited the example of Mondragón, I get this response: "Well that is because the Basque people are used to cooperatives. Worker-owned businesses wouldn't work here, in a strongly capitalist society." These cynics are surprised to learn about highly successful worker-owned businesses in the United States. In the San Francisco Bay Area, for example, there are many worker-owned businesses that are thriving. Alvarado Street Bakery in Petaluma, California, and the Arizmendi Bakeries located in six Bay Area cities have seen an increase in sales and profits even amidst an economic downturn. The principles underlying these cooperatives are the same as those practiced in Mondragón and not one of these worker-owners is Basque.

Scandinavian Models

Democratic government can facilitate the ability and opportunities for citizens to create fulfilling lives in cooperation with one another. Many of the most instructive examples exist today in Scandinavia.

Norwegian society is noted for its egalitarian culture and gender equality. The country has one of the highest standards of living in the world and boasts a highly developed social insurance system. Taxes are high, especially on high incomes, but the lack of poverty in Norway demonstrates the effectiveness of government programs that benefit from the contributions of its citizens. Education is free. Students do not leave college in debt.

Healthcare is free, as are hospital stays, medical tests, and surgeries.

Norway will pay a mother or father to stay home and care for a child. They have paid maternity and paternity leaves. Norway proves that when the economic system is structured to create more equality, poverty is nearly unknown. It is no surprise that in 2011, the UN Human Development Index declared Norway to be the world's happiest country. The four happiest countries are all situated in Northern Europe: Denmark, Norway, Finland, and the Netherlands, where government benefits are generous and reflect a substantive taxation policy.

Finland is another beacon of enlightened social systems. Free education, which includes free meals during school time, excellent pre-school programs, and highly innovative educational programs in high school and university, has led Finland to be known for having one of the best educational systems in the world. What emerges when education is so highly valued in a society is that it values life past the next quarter. In Helsinki, environmental concerns have top priority and the Finnish people are committed to lowering their carbon footprint. Seventy-five percent of Helsinki's daily commuters opt for public transportation.[45] Green building, energy efficiency, and the reduction of carbon emissions are incorporated into all city planning. Consequently, Helsinki received the top rank in the area of environmental politics in the European Green City Index. On their Embassy website, they define themselves as "an advanced industrial economy that has an extensive welfare state." They are proud of their social system. They don't cower from the word "welfare."

As Father Don Jose Maria Arizmendi, the founder of the Mondragón Cooperatives said, "The position that women have, in any society, is the exact measurement of its level of development." Finland was the first country where women were eligible to run in parliamentary elections (in 1906), before women even had the vote in the U.S. Today (2012), both the President and Prime Minister in Finland are women.

In Europe, and particularly in the Scandinavian countries, empathy is honored as part of the cultural landscape. The American mythos has promoted the lone hero, the rugged individual, with an endless frontier awaiting exploitation. Empathy is not a major theme in our culture. One problem with the libertarian myth, which builds on a rebellious and entitled individualism, is that it assumes endless frontiers and no limits to its aspirations. We live on a finite planet with finite resources. Managing this landscape takes maturity, discipline, and the ability to accept the reality of limits.

As Jeremy Rifkin notes, "The ability to recognize oneself in the other and other in oneself is a deeply democratizing experience. Empathy is the soul of democracy . . . The more empathic the culture, the more democratic its values and governing institutions."[46]

A civilization that values and practices empathy, that values and respects others and the environment, that values love before an abstract notion of liberty, will survive and survive well. We have models from which to learn. It is important that we learn from them with humility and gratitude.

"We need fewer prophets and more people who keep their word;
fewer utopians and more practical people."

—FATHER DON JOSÉ MARIA ARIZMENDI,
FOUNDER OF THE MONDRAGÓN COOPERATIVES

BIBLIOGRAPHY

Ehrenreich, Barbara. *Nickel and Dimed: On Not Getting By in America.* New York: Henry Holt, 2001.

Hartmann, Thom. *Threshold: The Crisis of Western Culture.* New York: Viking, the Penguin Group, 2009.

Hartmann, Thom. *The Progressive Plan to Pull American Back from the Brink,* New York, Plume, the Penguin Group, June 2010.

Kelly, Georgia. "An Alternative to Cutthroat Capitalism." *The Huffington Post.* October 12, 2010. www.huffingtonpost.com/georgia-kelly/an-alternative-to-cutthro_b_759546.html

Kelly, Georgia. "*Thrive*: Deconstructing the Film." *The Huffington Post.* December 28, 2011. www.huffingtonpost.com/georgia-kelly/thrive-film_b_1168930.html

Lakoff, George. *The Political Mind.* New York: The Penguin Group, 2008.

Lakoff, George. *Thinking Points*. New York: Farrar, Straus and Giroux, 2006

Rifkin, Jeremy. *The Empathic Civilization*. New York: Jeremy P. Tarcher/Penguin, 2009.

Jeffrey Sachs. "Libertarian Illusions." *The Huffington Post*. January 15, 2012. www.huffingtonpost.com/jeffrey-sachs/libertarian-illusions_b_1207878.html

Sachs, Jeffrey. *The Price of Civilization*, New York: Random House, 2011.

Sahtouris, Elisabet. *Earthdance: Living Systems in Evolution*, iUniverse, Inc., 2000.

Thrive website (solutions pages): www.thrivemovement.com/solutions-solutions_strategy

Thrive website (liberty pages): www.thrivemovement.com/solutions-liberty

Westen, Drew. *The Political Brain*. New York: Public Affairs, Perseus Books Group, 2007.

NOTES

31   Hazleton, Lesley. *The Right to Feel Bad*. New York: Doubleday, 1984.
32   www.freedomkentucky.org/index.php?title=Should_we_laugh_or_cry_when_Leno_goes_%27Jaywalking%27%3F
33   Krugman, Paul. "The Uneducated American," *The New York Times*. October 8, 2009.
34   Elizabeth Warren on Debt Crisis, Fair Taxation. October 2011, YouTube: www.youtube.com/watch?v=htX2usfqMEs
35   www.thrivemovement.com
36   www.youtube.com/watch?v=7QDv4sYwjO0
37   Hartmann, Thom. *Threshold: The Progressive Plan to Pull America Back from the Brink*. New York: The Penguin Group, 2009.
38   Pollitt, Katha. "Ron Paul's Strange Bedfellows." *The Nation*. January 5, 2012.
39   Dunham, Richard S. and Marinucci, Carla. "S.F. Billionaire Quietly Funds Paul Super PAC." *San Francisco Chronicle*. February 26, 2011.
40   "Sanders, Bernie."Sanders' Guide to Corporate Freeloaders." April 21, 2011. www.sanders.senate.gov/newsroom/news/?id=720371e9-b72e-4b7f-9b76-225ff8615fd6

41   Rooney, Ben. "Bank of America Cutting 30,000 jobs." *CNN Money.* September 12, 2011. www.money.cnn.com/2011/09/12/news/companies/bank_of_america_job_cuts/index.htm

42   Op. cit., Senator Bernie Sanders' Buide to Corporate Freeloaders.

43   Woodman, Spencer. "Labor Takes Aim at Walmart—Again." *The Nation.* January 23, 2012.

44   Clawson, Laura. *Daily Kos.* May 2, 2012. www.dailykos.com/story/2012/05/02/1088290/-Walmart-to-pay-more-than-4-8-million-in-back-wages-for-overtime-wage-theft

45   www.finland.org. Public/default.aspx?contentid=244809&nodeid=35833&culture=en-US

46   Rifkin, Jeremy. *The Empathic Civilization,* New York: Jeremy Tarcher/Penguin, New York, 2009, page 161.

CHAPTER THREE

TRANSCENDENTAL VANILLA PUDDING

By Ben Boyce

IN LATE 2011 and 2012, screenings of the documentary film *Thrive* were posted all over the San Francisco Bay Area. Clearly, there was a well-funded campaign to get this film into wide circulation. *Thrive* is a professionally produced documentary with high-end graphics, lots of sci-fi-type special effects, and numerous interviews with recognized progressive leaders and New Age human potential movement authors and lecturers. It has sufficient substance and potential cultural impact that it merits careful examination. The *Thrive* website claims that it has had over one million viewers, and that's one claim that I do believe. I enter into this critique with respect for the world from which it emerges and the audience for whom it is intended.

The initial viewing of the film left me with a residue of discomfort, but when Georgia Kelly, Director of Praxis Peace Institute, pointed to the website accompanying the documentary, this vague sense of uneasiness was magnified into full-fledged concern. A core group of Praxis members met to strategize how we would respond to this challenge. We recognized that *Thrive* had the capacity to insidiously insert right-wing libertarian ideology into the public discourse without most people realizing it. Consequently, we produced "Deconstructing Libertarianism," a pamphlet that was published online and is available on Praxis Peace Institute's website.[47] While this book broadens the focus to the larger issue of libertarianism, this chapter retains the focus on *Thrive* as an illustration of how a skillfully edited documentary, backed with a big budget, can draw new adherents to a long-discredited political doctrine.

More is involved than simply the film itself. The "Solutions" section of the *Thrive* website features quotations and headshots of Ayn Rand, Ron Paul, and Stefan Molyneux, with references to right-wing primary sources like Ludwig von Mises, Murray Rothbard, and other Austrian School "free market" economists. The Tea Party "Don't Tread on Me" emblem opens the "Liberty" chapter of the "Solutions" section.

These figures represent the ideological antithesis to the social democratic tradition that is the root of the progressive project. These are the very people that were cited approvingly by my ideological opponents when, as a young member of Students for a Democratic Society, I debated Young American for Freedom members at the local John Birch Society headquarters. It is unfortunate that the casual viewer of the film would not know the dark roots from which it draws sustenance. The *Thrive* website offers more clues.

We were not the only ones who felt a jolt of discomfort from viewing *Thrive* and then researching the accompanying website. At least ten of the leaders interviewed in the film felt that the true agenda of *Thrive* was not disclosed to them prior to release. One of the interview subjects, author John Robbins, wrote an article titled "Humanity and Sanity: Standing for a Thriving World (and challenging the Movie *Thrive*)"[48], in which he spoke for the other leaders who wanted to publicly disassociate themselves from the film:

Why have Amy Goodman, Deepak Chopra, Paul Hawken, Edgar Mitchell, Vandana Shiva, John Perkins, Elisabet Sahtouris, Duane Elgin, Adam Trombly, and yours truly, gone to the trouble of signing

*our names to this public statement? In my view, the deregulation of
the economy, and the demolition of government programs that Thrive
proposes, would take us even further in the direction of a winner-
take-all economy in which wealth would concentrate even more in
the hands of the financial elites.*

As one of the signers, evolutionary biologist Elisabet Sahtouris, writes:
"Without community, we do not exist, and community is about creating
relationships of mutual benefit. It does not just happen with flowers and
rainbows, and no taxes."

Many of the film's critics have focused on the questionable scientific
theories or the truly bizarre rehash of all the old *Protocols of the Elders of
Zion* conspiracy theories. I will leave the sinister conspiracy theories of
David Ickes, promoted in *Thrive,* for others to critique.

Thrive supports a radical transformation that would bring about a world
in which public schools, universities, the social safety net, and even basic
public infrastructures like roads and utilities have all been privatized.
Instead of police, we would have private security forces. As Foster Gamble,
creator of *Thrive,* states, "Private security works way better than the state"
(especially if they are hired to specifically protect just you and your entou-
rage). The civil court systems, which have provided the foundation for justice for the Anglo-American civilization since the Magna Carta, would be
abolished in favor of private courts, in which competing legal claims would
be adjusted against our personal legal insurance. The outcomes might be
less desirable if you can't afford your private legal insurance bill.

Foster Gamble claims, naively in my view, that he has no political
agenda, but his ideal society, arrived at through a series of stages, would
be a libertarian utopia in which there would be no taxes, no public sector
services, no unions, no Social Security or Medicare, and eventually no
government, and virtually everything would be privately owned, including the streets we drive on.

"It's clear that when you drive into a shopping center you are on a
private road, and almost without exception it is in great shape," explains

the *Thrive* website, failing to note the systematic disinvestment in the public sector infrastructure that adherents of this anti-tax, anti-government
ideology have subjected us to for decades. Our public roads, along with
the entire national physical infrastructure, as well as our social services
and public sector healthcare, have suffered from this disinvestment. Gamble's quaint insistence that there is no political agenda is based on a very
limited and skewed understanding of the actual power relationships that
determine the shape of the world we are compelled to live in. He has no
analysis of the determinative role of the corporate sector as the primary
source of political power, and this makes his grand theory of the stages of
global transformation groundless.

The animating principle of the *Thrive* doctrine is the conviction that
the fundamental principle on which modern civilization was founded,
a democratically elected government working on behalf of the common
good, funded by taxes, is a form of vile tyranny contrary to the peculiar
moral axioms promoted by *Thrive*. Here is one among many astounding quotes from the website: **"If it is against life itself to violate another
against their will, then our very 'Democracy'—which is born of and
sustains itself by taking people's hard-earned money, whether they like
it or not, and calling it 'taxation,'—is, in and of itself, a *violation*."**

It seems appropriate to raise a red flag and signal awareness of the
neo-libertarian values that are at the heart of the film, so when the topic
of *Thrive* comes up, controversy will arise alongside it. Given the stakes
in the rise of a virulent conservative movement that has adopted large
chunks of the libertarian agenda, and the emergence of a powerful worldwide Occupy movement that wants to take back public space and reclaim
our democracy, the time of political reckoning is at hand, so we can no
longer afford to waste our time with distractions, sideshows, and ideological dead-ends.

The importance of addressing the political ideology underlying the film
has been heightened by the number of New Age adherents who are drawn
to it, attracted by the tone and style, the high production values, and the
delicious implication that they are being let in on a civilization-changing

secret. Progressive movement activists are appalled that when the New Age cohort (and, sadly, a significant element within the Occupy movement) do finally get politically engaged, it is under the auspices of the highly questionable and historically discredited libertarian political philosophy at the core of *Thrive*.

Make no mistake, the actual policy solutions that are hinted at in the documentary, and more explicitly described on the *Thrive* website, constituted the norm in the first Gilded Age of "laissez faire" capitalism, the McKinley Era at the end of the nineteenth century, for which the libertarian/conservative movements seem to still pine. That was a time when there were minimal taxes on corporations, no taxes on the wealthy to support social services, no worker's rights, no pesky EPA environmental regulations, no minimum wage, no social safety net to prevent families from tumbling precipitously from marginal employment and insecure housing to abject penury and homelessness. This was the world created by raw, unchecked capitalism, Blake's "satanic mills" of social Darwinist exploitation of the masses. It was in response to this affront to the dignity of humanity that the modern progressive movement arose. We are still engaged in that struggle to this very day, as we seek to cast off the shackles of corporate domination of our lives and our political system. *Thrive* is not the medicine for that disease, it is a stronger dose of the same poison.

This was the dystopian, savagely unjust world that the courageous pioneers of the progressive movement banded together to address in a historical movement that can be dated from the French and American revolutions, which established the rights of citizenship, democratic self-governance, and the values of "*liberte, egalite, fraternite.*" This new vision was given intellectual form in the international federations that sprang up in the wake of the epochal revolutions in Europe in 1848, moving in an unbroken arc to the present day. The global revolution that we and our ancestors have sought in this historic transformational struggle is still only a partially realized promise.

Thrive is *not* the next step in this unfinished revolution. In fact, its ideological core, when all the New Age smoke-and-mirrors and special effects are stripped away, is Ayn Randian neo-libertarianism, an adolescent dream of a Nietzschean world of self-appointed overlords without social limits or legal constraints. What the program of *Thrive* would actually amount to in practice is to complete the long slide into a corporatocracy, ruled by a corrupt oligarchy that has severed its sense of social affiliation with the 99 percent, whom they exploit as expendable commodities. The implementation of the *Thrive* program would serve as a shock doctrine to tighten their social Darwinist tourniquet on what's left of the public commons in order to increase their share of the take. The radical dismantling of the public sector in favor of privatized arrangements would inevitably concentrate the remaining wealth in the hands of the already rich. That's the historical reality that this doctrine actually delivers, not the cotton candy utopian fantasy of a fully privatized society without courts, government, or taxes that *Thrive* spins. History has already delivered that verdict.

Everywhere in the world where the libertarian ideology has been put into practice, the condition of mass immiseration of the working class and concentration of wealth in the hands of the one percent ruling elite has been a consistent historical fact. It has been tried and failed. If you want to see a contemporary case study, look to Pinochet's Chile, in which a nascent socialist experiment was ruthlessly crushed, and in the ensuing panic and social confusion, a radical reordering of the economic system, a kind of shock doctrine, was rammed through on a dazed and demoralized population. Chile was the poster child for the Chicago School of "free market" economics (which was the American successor to the Austrian School), and that model was imposed on many other countries that had the misfortune to be forced into IMF and World Bank "structural adjustment" programs. The net effect was to destroy any sources of mass social and economic power, such as indigenous cottage industries and trade unions, so that the only power left standing was the corporation, represented by their political front groups, and enforced by a private militia at the service of the oligarchs. The state and the corporate oligarchy were fused, and all competing centers of power neutralized. That is the actual historical endgame for the libertarian project. The trajectory is consistent across the world. This will not lead to the era of prosperity and personal freedom promised in *Thrive*.

We are still recovering from the latest crisis consequent to a thirty-year spree of unregulated capitalism of the kind touted in libertarian economic doctrine. One would think the recent global economic collapse would have finally buried the quaint notion that markets are self-regulating. Even the high priest of free market fundamentalist economic orthodoxy, former Fed Chair Alan Greenspan, a devoted Ayn Rand libertarian, recanted publicly on this point. He testified before Congress in 2008, as the ashes were still falling from the ceiling in the aftermath of the bonfire incinerating the wealth of an entire generation: "Our model could not comprehend this outcome..." This religion should be dead. Only plutocratic money keeps it alive.

To be fair, we can extract from the neo-libertarian ideology the useful seed teaching on the importance of the value of individual liberty and a healthy concern for privacy rights, but we should make it clear that the policy prescriptions in the "Solutions" section of *Thrive* are reactionary and inadequate to the great task of the twenty-first century. That monumental task is to work—individually and collectively—to build up our environmental and social capital through re-structuring an integrated network of energy grids, transit systems, and workforce housing. The environmental imperative is to reduce global greenhouse gas levels and draw down energy intensity. We need a full employment economy, accompanied by fully-funded vocational training, which sets millions of young people on the path to a stable family life and gives hope and purpose to economically marginal citizens. There is a desperate need to develop the social and political will to put the people to work doing the essential tasks of environmental remediation, public works infra-structure projects, childcare and teaching, nursing and caretaking. This will take money and political commitment in the form of public and private organizations, funded through fair taxes and voluntary donations.

Such change cannot happen solely on the basis of the private market system or the nonprofit sector. The agency of national governments cooperating in closely knit international institutions will be required in order to scale up the resources to actually accomplish this task. It is incoherent and ahistorical to believe we can defend and enhance the common good without collective action and the instrument of government. In communications from Foster Gamble since the first draft of this article, he seems clueless about the actual political implications of the clearly libertarian foundations of the *Thrive* project. He wants to deny that *Thrive* has a political agenda, which is risible.

My colleague Benjamin Colby has drawn out a logical schematic of the four fundamental ideological poles, and makes it clear that you can't occupy all four quadrants simultaneously. Mr. Gamble claims to have arrived at a magical synthesis of conservative, liberal, libertarian, and socialist elements in his grand design outlined in *Thrive*. Let's get real! Some things come down to "A or not A." Touting a kind of magical thinking, in which all the opposites are somehow mystically reconciled in some kind of transcendental vanilla pudding is profoundly unrealistic. The plain answer is that it is incoherent, and intellectually honest people have to call a spade a spade.

The *Thrive* message must be publicly repudiated because it could perform essentially the same function that the "New Age" movement did in the 1970s, which was to dissipate the revolutionary energies of the political and cultural awakening of the '60s and remove an entire generation from the field of political struggle and the progressive movement for social and ecological justice. Instead, it directed them to put their energies in "spiritual quests," "self-realization," personal fulfillment, and privatized concerns disconnected from a sense of social and historical responsibility. We have paid a dear price for that loss of collective historical consciousness.

With the field cleared, the well-organized and well-funded forces of the nascent right-wing conservative movement moved in to fill the vacuum, while the well-meaning spiritual seekers attended to their "personal development" or their "spiritual path." Meanwhile, the material conditions that permitted them the luxury of disengaging from political life were being steadily undermined by the corporate imperative to concentrate wealth in the hands of the one percent ownership class. Now, many of these New Age folks are finding that their sources of income as cultural creatives have dried up, as our corporate overlords have finally deemed their class to be superfluous. The boot heel is now on *their* neck. Their abdication of historical responsibility helped enable the dire condition in which we now find ourselves. Let's not let the forces behind *Thrive* derail the next generation of potential leaders of the worldwide progressive movement.

We can agree on some basic points. The sociopathic, social Darwinist bent that the modern Tea Party-dominated Republican Party has taken is frightening and potentially fatal to a free society, even to the survival of the species. The dysfunctional, sold-out centrist core of the Democratic Party is totally inadequate to the historical moment, not to mention even to the basic political task of fending off the aggressive Republican media attack machine. We can agree that we need something better. But it is definitely not the warmed over neo-libertarianism that is the baseline political foundation of *Thrive*.

Would that Gamble takes *Thrive* back into the shop for an edit, revisits the "Solutions" section, and returns to the opening promise of the film. We have in common the search for new sources of energy, food safety from GMOs (genetically modified organisms), and the project of re-tooling industrial civilization for a steady-state sustainable future that delivers personal freedom and the resources with which to enjoy it. We may share the goal, but we do differ deeply on the method.

WEBSITES

www.transitionculture.org/2012/01/09/film-review-why-thrive-is-best-avoided

www.santacruz.com/news/2012/03/13/the_right_libertarian_agenda_at_the_heart_of_thrive

www.charleseisenstein.net/essays/thrive-the-story-is-wrong-but-the-spirit-is-right/

www.huffingtonpost.com/georgia-kelly/thrive-film_b_1168930.html

www.thrivedebunked.wordpress.com/

NOTES

47 www.praxispeace.org; www.praxispeace.org/pdf/DL_020612.pdf

48 Robbins, John. "Humanity and Sanity: Standing for a Thriving World (and challenging the Movie *Thrive*)." March 2012. www.praxispeace.org

CHAPTER FOUR

TURNING THE TABLES: THE PATHOLOGIES AND UNREALIZED PROMISE OF LIBERTARIANISM

By Gus diZerega

CHIP PY, A longtime resident of Silver Spring, Maryland, was walking downtown after eating lunch there. He took out his camera and started to photograph the contrast between the tops of the office buildings and the blue sky.

Within seconds, a private security guard informed Py that picture-taking was not permitted there. In his report of the episode, Marc Fisher of the *Washington Post* quoted Py, "I am on a city street, in a public place . . . taking pictures is a right that I have, protected by the First Amendment."[49]

The guard informed him he was on private property and sent Py to the office of the developer that built the new downtown. The *Post* article elaborated, "There, marketing official Stacy Horan told Py that although Ellsworth Drive—where many of the downtown's shops and eateries are located—may look like a public street, it is actually treated as private property, controlled by Peterson." It had in fact been a public street, until the county "privatized" it.

From a libertarian perspective, Py's experience is an example of "freedom" at work, and public places where the First Amendment applies are areas of governmental exploitation and oppression. How could an ideology of freedom end up with a world where, if libertarians had their way, the First Amendment would not apply *anywhere* because all public spaces will have been privatized under the arbitrary control of an owner?

In a time when American politics has become largely a morass of nihilism, corruption, and debased public debate, libertarian candidates such as Ron Paul stand out seductively. They speak claiming a strong moral foundation, they believe ideas matter, and they are willing to say the would-be emperors within both parties are without the virtues they claim to embody. It is hard not to be drawn into sympathy with these libertarians even when we find ourselves at odds over important political issues. These people at least stand for something. In a world where few people of public importance stand for anything beyond enlarging their pocketbooks and power, that is indeed impressive. But is it enough? What about the rest?

The rest is both much less and much more than libertarians claim.

WHAT IS LIBERTARIANISM?

At its core, libertarianism is the belief that "free markets" provide the optimal framework within which all human interaction should take place. Some grant a small additional role for government as a "night watchman state" to enforce contracts and deal with violent crime and defense. Others think markets can do even those tasks.

Very importantly, most libertarians draw their conclusions from a radically individualistic moral philosophy and argue that no peaceful individuals can be justifiably aggressed against. As Ayn Rand put it, "No man has the right to initiate the use of physical force against others."[50] It is this moral foundation that makes them such staunch defenders of civil liberties for individuals and critics of war. Their additional defense of the "free market" arises from their belief that markets simply reflect the choices peaceful people make when they cooperate with one another. Yet, for many of us, something seems deeply inadequate to the libertarian claims that their nonaggression principle justifies laissez faire capitalism and relegates government to a purely supportive role for maintaining a good business environment. We are attracted by their paeans to individualism, their praise of responsibility and individual initiative, and their opposition to those eager to force us to live the way they demand. And yet *something* seems to be lacking, even if we have a hard time putting our finger on it.

We skeptics are right. Their terminology uses common words in uncommonly narrow ways. Their faulty idea of an individual, combined with their narrow interpretation of "nonaggression," leads libertarians to misunderstand what private property is. Along with "nonaggression" and the "individual," "private property" is *the* core principle underlying libertarianism's solutions to all of society's major problems.

Once libertarian framing of what constitutes individuals and aggression are accepted, arbitrary assumptions embedded within their arguments take away our ability to conceptualize what bothers us. Political theory becomes a source of blindness rather than insight. Libertarians give terms such as "individual," "aggression," and "property" arbitrarily narrow meanings. Starting with a fragmentary understanding of their key concepts, their arguments ultimately provide cover for oppressing individuals and masking many forms of aggression. An ideology of freedom becomes in practice something quite different.

Growing out of these misunderstandings of the terms "individual," "aggression," and "private property," another problem arises that renders libertarians unable to comprehend the nature and value of political democracy. These are serious shortcomings for an ideology claiming to respect individuals, honor property rights, and criticize government abuses.

And yet, if genuinely understood, the libertarians' principle of nonaggression helps guide us toward a revival in the quality of American public life and public debate from its present debased form. In other words, my critique does not reject their principles; it argues that libertarians *do not understand them.* When properly understood, their principles do outline a vision of a genuinely free and prosperous society.

INDIVIDUALS

Libertarians consider individuals to be a kind of social atom, the basic building blocks from which more complex social institutions arise. All of our complex institutions, from language and custom to governments and corporations, can ultimately be traced back to the actions of individuals. Therefore, if individuals are not aggressed against, the institutions arising from their cooperation will also be beneficent.

This view distinguishes libertarians from traditional conservatives who, from Edmund Burke to William Buckley, emphasize that we are embedded within networks of tradition and custom that require honoring our ancestors, respecting what survived from the past, and protecting our cultural inheritance for future generations. It also distinguishes libertarians from most liberals and progressives, who argue that because our cultural and social relations so powerfully shape who we are—either inhibiting or expanding human well-being—we should seek to overcome and eventually replace all institutions of domination and arbitrary power.

Both genuine conservatives and progressives view people as embedded within a thick context of social relations. What distinguishes them from one another is that conservatives emphasize that what has survived has stood the test of time and should be changed only slowly, and progressives believe that as we better understand this context, we can abolish institutions that perpetuate or create new forms of oppression and domination.

Libertarians sometimes pay lip service to insights from both perspectives, but they focus overwhelmingly on the individual as an isolated entity. They assert that through voluntary cooperation with one another, individuals can create a prosperous, free, and creative society where all people are free to live, so long as they do not violate another. There is obviously considerable truth to this libertarian claim *in some contexts*. The libertarian error comes from seeking to include all relevant dimensions of human life within these partial contexts.

IT USUALLY BEGINS WITH AYN RAND

While the libertarian tradition has a number of key intellectual ancestors, today Ayn Rand towers over the others in influence and in number
of readers. This section's heading repeats the title of Jerome Tucille's history of the libertarian movement,[51] written during the time of its initial
expansion from small groups able to meet in the private homes of people
like Rand and Murray Rothbard, to its present nation-wide scale.[52] Today,
more than fifty years after her books first emerged, Rand's writings continue to sell in the hundreds of thousands, with over twelve million of her
books in print.[53]

Ayn Rand's influence extends well beyond self-consciously libertarian Americans and, in the process, magnifies libertarianism's influence
far beyond those who adopted the term to define themselves. A 1991
survey conducted by the Library of Congress and Book-of-the-Month
Club discovered that more Americans reported *Atlas Shrugged* had
influenced their lives over any other title except for the Bible.[54] Many
of those now calling themselves "conservatives" owe more to Ayn Rand
than to traditional conservative thinkers. Alan Greenspan and Paul
Ryan admit to having been significantly influenced by Rand. Glenn
Beck and other so-called Christian conservatives sound more like Ayn
Rand when it comes to the poor and unfortunate than anything written
in the Gospels.

Ayn Rand has long been popular among young people struggling to
define themselves in a society that increasingly seeks to narrow their
horizons and diminish control over their own lives. Rand's depiction
of strong creative individuals standing firm in their visions of how life
should be lived can be inspiring reading for young people discovering
the many hypocrisies in our society. She exposes how the lust for power
hides behind supposedly noble motives and skewers the claims of those
wielding power that they only act for the good of others. When many of
us first encountered her, we were just beginning to suspect these truths
and recognize that many people's actions had little connection to their

words. Rand's fiction gave us a framework for understanding this reality and encouraged us to vow not to do such things ourselves.

As an older teenager, I certainly enjoyed *The Fountainhead* and *Atlas Shrugged*. These novels served as a kind of bracing literary tonic to help me say "no" as best I could to such pressures. I was hardly alone. She helped some of us overcome the fear of not fitting in and gave us permission to walk in step with our own drummer. In that way, she assisted us in living life with greater integrity. This is Ayn Rand's positive side, and I think it is very important.

If this was the only aspect to Rand's celebration of the individual, she would rightly be praised as one of the greatest twentieth century literary forces for defending human freedom. Unfortunately, it was not.

Rand's striking fictional characters exhibit her theory of what human beings truly are. This is a theory with many of its roots based on her early fascination with the German philosopher Friedrich Nietzsche, and in particular with his division of humanity into "supermen," an aristocracy of virtue and ability, and the inferior people who resented their excellence. In varying degrees, this basic dichotomy stayed with her to the end. For example, in *Atlas Shrugged* her ideal man, John Galt, said:

> *The man at the top of the intellectual pyramid contributes the most to all below him, but gets nothing except his material payment, receiving no intellectual bonus from others to add to the value of his time. The man at the bottom who, left to himself, would starve in his hopeless ineptitude, contributes nothing to those above him, but receives the bonus of all their brains. Such is the nature of the "competition" between the strong and weak of intellect.*[55]

Beyond his praise of creativity, Galt's description of superior and inferior human beings carries four additional characteristics that remained part of Rand's outlook, and have powerfully influenced subsequent libertarian thinking.

First, the individual is radically atomistic. Superiority arises from those with better intellect, and intellect is self-contained. In explaining her concept of man, Rand wrote, "man is a heroic being, with his own happiness as the moral purpose of his life, with productive achievement as his noblest activity, and his reason as his only absolute."[56] Essentially, John Galt is treated as completely autonomous throughout the novel. Like a Greek God he is a force of nature, albeit a mortal one.

Second, virtue and excellence ultimately exist along a single continuum. As Galt explained, "Thinking is man's only basic virtue, from which all others proceed."[57] For Rand, ideally every dimension of a person's life was evaluated by, and subordinated to, reason.

Third, the greatest number of people is incompetent to live their lives unassisted by the creativity and ability of the elite. As Ludwig von Mises, the economist who did the most to strengthen libertarianism's grounding in free market economics, wrote to her: "You have the courage to tell the masses what no politician told them: you are inferior and all the improvements in your conditions which you simply take for granted you owe to the effort of men who are better than you."[58] She is describing a human *pyramid* and pyramids are biggest along their bottom. Absent this pyramid, the entire premise of *Atlas Shrugged* dissolves into absurdity.

Fourth and finally, the pay-off from the less rational to the more rational is measured only in "material payment." The market is therefore the proper way to evaluate the relative worth of a person's contribution to society. In this last point, Rand has amalgamated the Nietzschean superman with the successful businessman and rendered it the most perfect exemplar, a theme absent in as *The Fountainhead*. To be sure, those who "shrugged" in her novel included artists and inventors, but they are vital primarily to a society's future, not its present.

No individual resembles Rand's image of complete self-sufficiency. As Rand's own biographies demonstrate, she was powerfully impacted in her childhood by a vastly less-than-loving mother. Her youth in viciously anti-Semitic Czarist Russia and her young adult years lived during the horrors of the Russian Revolution had a powerful impact on her views of human beings. At the same time she often benefited in crucial ways from the kindness of others both in Russia and during the years of her emigration and gradual rise to success in the United States. Later in life, she was powerfully and emotionally impacted by critics' and others' reactions to her works. Ayn Rand cared, even when she said she didn't. Like every person, Ayn Rand's life reflected the complex interweaving of her own abilities, the people she met, the times in which she lived, and the unpredictable play of luck and fate, all coming together in an act of co-creation. Rand created a world and in turn was created by it.

Her image of a few supermen and women surrounded by vast numbers of the less competent and even more of the truly incompetent is not true. If her biographers are correct, her intense elitism likely came from growing up Jewish in the Czarist autocracy with its state sponsored pogroms, followed by the mob actions of the Russian Revolution. Under Czarist autocracy, hundreds of years of despotism had left most Russians incapable of acting responsibly outside their most intimate circles. Rand's view of coercion as physical force represents the experience of a person raised in such violent societies. It left her relatively numb to the other forms aggression could take.

DISAPPEARING INDIVIDUALISM

There is a fatal tension between Rand's emphasis in *The Fountainhead* on independence, initiative, and love of one's work as determining a person's worth (like the architect Howard Roark) and John Galt's later claim in *Atlas Shrugged* that reason is the ultimate standard of human excellence.

The *Fountainhead* suggests a multiplicity of excellences based on internal standards of creativity whereas the second suggests a single scalar. Roark is first and foremost an artistic creator, and hardly financially successful or even financially motivated. There are innumerable possible artistic creators, each following their own visions. But reason is a single scale, and as Rand's philosophy developed, there appeared to be only one rational way to live a life, her way. Over time, individual creativity became subordinate to her concept of rationality, proceeding from supposedly universally correct premises.

After his encounter with Rand and her closest students, Murray Rothbard, another major figure in the history of libertarian thought, identified the biggest problem at the core of Rand's idea of individualism. Rothbard concluded that Rand's philosophy did not lead to valuing the individual. Quite the contrary. As he put it, "she actually denies all individuality whatsoever." Rand's exaltation of reason as man's highest and most definitive characteristic meant that she regarded emotion as subject to reason. Men were only "bundles of premises" and their virtue or vice depended on whether they had the right premises. To be rational, people's choices had to rest on rational premises, of which there was only one set, those Rand taught. She told Rothbard, "I could be just as good in music as in economics if I applied myself." Rothbard concluded that for Rand the perfect society "would be a place where all men were identical, in their souls if not their personal appearance." [59] As he wrote, "Since [her followers] all have the same premises, they are all . . . individual parts in a machine." [60] (As we shall see, Rothbard did not free himself from another version of this problem.)

Jennifer Burns and Ann Heller's excellent biographies emphasize the extraordinary conformity in dress, manners, hairstyles, and even smoking habits of Rand's inner circle. Rachmaninoff's romantic music was good, but composers such as Beethoven or Brahms were bad. Because he depicted everything in stark black and white terms, Micky Spillane's mysteries were examples of the best literature. Books by people with whom Rand had had a falling out were actually prohibited from being read by students who wanted to be close to her. Even advocates of individualism and free markets were judged so unacceptable that her students were forbidden to socialize with them. After their falling out, Nathaniel Brandon, long Rand's right hand man, described the pressures for absolute conformity he imposed on those who wished to study with her. [61] At one point, Rand decreed that only she and Nathaniel and Barbara Brandon could legitimately be termed "Objectivists." Everyone else who followed her teachings could at most be termed a "student of Objectivism."

This is in remarkable contrast with the message she taught in *The Fountainhead*, where she distinguished between those who followed their own ideas and values and those she labeled "second-handers."[62] Howard Roark describes them: "Their ability is not within them, but somewhere in that space which divides one human body from another. Not an entity but a relation. The second-hander acts, but the source of his actions is scattered in every other living person."[63] [64] There are two ironies here. First, every person, even Ayn Rand, is who they are because of their relations with others. But second, all those she accepted for study had to endorse being "second-handers" to the point where they *gave up* their independent stance to think for themselves. Rand *required* that those who came to study with her be *and remain* second-handers. Perhaps this is why she once observed, "I thought that my fans disappointed and depressed me worse than my enemies."[65] No one with a mind securely their own could stay in such an environment.

Not all libertarians are so slavishly devoted to Rand's ideas. But to my knowledge, all have internalized some version of this failure to understand the very individuality they praise. If they have not internalized a model of the individual that cannot appreciate individuality, they internalize a model of the market that subordinates individuality to the dictates of the price mechanism. This was Murray Rothbard's failing, for he regarded the free market as a perfect reflection of the choices free men and women made when choosing to interact voluntarily. Therefore, interventions by government that changed the rule or injected values the market did not serve were always a sign of violence and oppression.

COERCION BY THE MARKET

To understand Rothbard's unknowing rejection of individuality, we need to look briefly at how markets work. The market does not simply reflect the free choices of human beings. The market effectively coordinates a worldwide network of exchange because it radically simplifies every exchange into monetary terms. Supposedly, I do not need to know anything but a product's price to decide whether I am better or worse off by buying it. This quality can empower individuals and/or subordinate them, as surely as the most detailed governmental regulations, depending on context.

When free men and women look at prices, they serve as signals, telling them what they must part with in order to obtain something they want. It remains their choice whether they do so or not. Prices are one factor among many when we decide what to do. Individual business people, partnerships, and families all operate within such an environment. So do many who work for others. At this level markets can empower both producers and consumers. But, this is not the only level at which the market operates.

Consider a corporation. Here strangers buy shares in a common enterprise, hoping to gain returns on their investment. Sometimes, there are millions of shareholders. Today shareholders might own shares of mutual funds, and these funds invest in companies from which they expect good returns. Under such circumstances no one has much individual influence on how a corporation acts, and because many invest in mutual funds, often they do not know what corporations they "own."

Another prominent libertarian economist, Milton Friedman, famously argued that corporate managers do not own their companies. They are employees of those who do. Consequently, if they act in any way that reduces returns to owners in order to serve other values, they are stealing from their employers.[66]

But who are their employers? Friedman argued the shareholders were. But we have already seen that most shareholders do not exercise any power over the use of their resources by a firm, and often do not even know what firms they "own." Let's imagine that one of these shareholder "owners" notices that the company in which they hold shares is acting unethically. They will be unable to change its actions because they "own" such a tiny portion of the whole, and so perhaps they decide to sell their shares in protest.

Shares sold by people objecting to what they regarded as unethical behavior would be purchased by others who are either ignorant of what was happening or who did not care. The more shares are sold in protest, the bigger the financial gains for those who then buy them. Knowledgeable buyers with fewer scruples will buy additional shares, anticipating an even greater return for themselves from the unethical behavior than would have been the case had no one sold. When apartheid prevailed, many progressive groups urged divestment from companies doing business in South Africa. One argument given against this strategy was that the shares would simply be purchased by others with fewer scruples.

If unethical behavior is profitable, selling shares exacts a financial loss on ethical shareholders while enabling less ethical or knowledgeable shareholders to make a greater financial gain! Selling a share for ethical reasons does not increase the pressure to change the objectionable behavior and can even strengthen its continuance if it is bought by a less ethical investor. This kind of "ownership" *penalizes* ethical behavior and rewards the opposite so long as it is profitable. It is the *opposite* of what we normally mean when we say someone "owns" something.

If, despite Milton Friedman's admonitions, a CEO decides to sacrifice profits for some ethical goal that decision will be reflected in a lower share price than would otherwise be the case. If it is low enough to be noticed, the CEO is likely to be ousted in an unfriendly takeover bid by others less ethically motivated. So the CEO does not really control corporate property any more than the shareholders do.

A primary characteristic of ownership is control over what is owned. Neither shareholders nor CEOs ultimately control a corporation. No human being does. Theoretically a corporation, like the market, is immortal while individual shareholders and corporate and investment managers come and go. *In capitalism individual ownership has been replaced by market ownership.*

Corporations are as responsive to market dictates as a human-created institution can be. The market dominates what companies do on pain of their being taken over by other companies operating in even greater harmony with market incentives. Like CEOs, shareholders work for the capitalist system. Their job is to shift capital to where it will bring the greatest

money profit, and their fee for doing their job well is the profit they make
in their stock. Managers who serve other values are ejected, and so are
shareholders who put values other than profit first. "Ownership" has
shifted from individuals to the capitalist system, and rather than enhanc-
ing individual freedom, the system now requires individuals to serve its
values on pain of gradually or quickly losing their fee for managing its
assets, to be replaced by "better" employees.

The profits shareholders make for investing wisely are the fee the market provides so that its property is well managed, just as corporate managers obtain a fee for competently managing property they do not own.
Whereas individual ownership is used in myriad ways, reflecting the richness, strengths, and weaknesses of the human character, market "ownership" serves much narrower values. In capitalism, organizations respond
to prices, real and anticipated, and to nothing else. In the process, the
concept of moral responsibility traditionally entailed in the concept of
ownership has disappeared.

Economists have internalized libertarian ideas about individuals and
the market more than in any other profession. This is because if every
individual acted like a rational sociopath the market would operate as it
now does. Individuals do not usually act this way, but the market creates
a context that narrows the power of human values to influence anything
but the final product. So "sociopathic" models of "rational choice" work in
economic theory even if not in human life.

Our present wholesale collapse in business ethics illustrates this dehu-
manizing process. Today many corporations have pretty much freed themselves from the world of human values whereas privately held companies
remain a part of civil society, still existing within the realm of freedom.
Koch Industries is privately held, and as a consequence Charles and David
Koch can legitimately be considered responsible for its actions, good and
bad alike. They committed massive fraud against Native Americans and
these actions are a permanent blot on their character.[67] On the other hand,
if General Electric (GE) does something good or bad, as a tiny owner of
GE stock I can reap neither praise nor blame, even when that praise or

blame is attenuated to reflect the percentage of shares I own. I have as much influence over GE as I do over Apple, where, to my knowledge, I own no shares at all.

The libertarian equation of the market as the vehicle for expressing individual freedom sacrifices all individuality that does not serve corporate profit. Neither shareholders nor management are truly free. Prices have become commands. What does not make a profit does not get done. Even Murray Rothbard, who perceptively saw problems in Ayn Rand's vision of the individual, ultimately was no more a defender of individuality than she.

But how, then, are we to think about individuals and why they are so important?

THINKING ABOUT INDIVIDUALS AS THEY ARE

In some sense we are unique individuals. Clearly, we are also beings decisively shaped by time, place, and the key experiences of our lives. How do we make sense of how these seemingly disparate characteristics relate to one another? And why are individuals so uniquely valuable? I think sociologists Peter Berger and Thomas Luckmann give a good start for answering these questions. As they explain it, to understand what an individual is, we need to keep at least three perspectives simultaneously in mind. These perspectives *cannot* be reduced to one or the other.[68]

1. *Society is created by the actions of individuals.* Ayn Rand's model fits easily here and, in fact, this is the almost universal libertarian view. Individuals are social atoms whose combinations create society. The best society is one where these combinations are voluntary. As Rand put it, "The principle of trade is the only rational ethical principle for all human relationships, personal and social, private and public, spiritual and material. It is the principle of justice."[69] This point is important and true as far as it goes, but it does not go nearly as far as Rand or other libertarians think it does.

2. *Individuals are social creations.* We reflect our place and time. We even think with concepts we inherit and only slightly modify. Albert Einstein could never have arisen on the Lakota Reservation, nor could Lakota medicine person Black Elk have become the man he was in late nineteenth century central Europe. Even intensely personal behavior, such as suicide, varies in frequency from society to society. I suspect we can all name encounters with others that decisively shaped who we have become.

3. *Society is encountered by individuals as an objective reality.* This third point is a little more difficult to grasp. We are born knowing nothing or next to nothing about our world. Newborns become fully-fledged members of their society by learning how members of that society make sense of things, and adopting all or most of it for themselves. Their consciousness reflects that social world of meanings within which they live as surely as it reflects knowledge about the physical world. Initially, we take as unquestionably true both the things we learn about the material world—rocks are hard, stoves are hot— and the things we learn about the social world—marriage is between a man and a woman, or in other societies that marriage is between one man and many women. Today some children are learning that their parents can share the same gender.

Beginning in infancy, the child encounters a socially mediated reality, we are not simply the products of our environment. To some degree we can stand outside and question what we once took as simply natural. The child notices how two messages he receives do not fit together, and so he separates himself to some degree from both in order to evaluate this contradiction. This process continues into adulthood. But there is no place where we can stand outside all of our socially acquired knowledge and evaluate it all at once. No matter how sophisticated our questions, we always ask them within a social context that remains largely taken for granted.

In this important sense a human life is a creative discovery process where we continually encounter that which we do not know from within a context of what we think we do know. If we are honest and not afraid, we will recognize that the edges of what we think we know blends into what we know we do not know. The lines are blurred and how we ultimately interpret them can potentially send unexpected shock waves deep into our taken-for-granted world of certainty. But we can never doubt everything.

Berger and Luckmann argued, and I think correctly, "Society is a human product. Society is an objective reality. Man is a social product. An analysis that leaves out any one of these three moments will be distortive. Only with the transmission of the social world to a new generation (that is, internalization as effectuated by socialization) does the fundamental social dialectic appear in its totality."[70] These three dimensions do not exist in a linear causal relationship to one another. *They are always simultaneous,* creating an enduring and dynamic pattern of relationships out of which both individuals and societies emerge.[71]

THE CENTRALITY OF RELATIONSHIP

This insight tells us that *individuals cannot be separated from their relationships* because our relationships are fundamental in determining who we are. As we make sense of our relationships and encounters within the world we inherited, we must interpret what happens to us. We are unavoidably creative as we give them a meaning that is always at least to some degree unique to ourselves. I believe another Russian, Yevgeny Yevtushenko, captured a core insight about what an individual is far better than has Rand or any libertarian I have ever read.

In any man who dies there dies with him
his first snow and kiss and fight.
It goes with him.

There are left books and bridges
and painted canvas and machinery.
Whose fate is to survive.

But what has gone is also not nothing:
by the rule of the game something has gone.
Not people die but worlds die in them.[72]

In a word, individuals are creative gestalts formed from interacting relationships, and every relationship involves at least two parties. Think of the well-known image of two faces, which, looked at differently, reveals a vase. The vase is dependent on the faces, the faces dependent on the vase. Different faces manifest different vases, and vice versa.

Every such gestalt is a unique center of consciousness, a self constituting the only real center of moral action. We are unique selves *because* of our relationships. If there are no relationships, there are no individuals.

This observation is paradoxical, but it is not nonsensical. Physicists deal with a somewhat similar paradox at the core of their knowledge. Consider the photon, a genuinely quantum phenomenon. In quantum mechanics a photon is a single quantum, and as such it is far more paradoxical than any comparatively gigantic atom. Atoms are things in ways that photons are not. Thinking about quanta helps us think more clearly about individuals than does using the libertarian image of an atom.

Ask certain experimental questions about the nature of light, and photons act as if they were particles (individuals). Ask other questions, and they act as if they were waves (certainly not individuals). *A photon is at least both* even though our minds cannot conceive clearly how this can be. The math works and exceedingly exact predictions can be made, but a clear mental image of what a photon really is eludes us.

Individuals only resemble atoms (particles) in some contexts and when some questions are asked of us. Ask an individual one set of questions and you get answers in keeping with libertarian beliefs, where individuals to some degree resemble irreducible units of social and moral reality. Do you want to be an engineer or a physicist or an artist? Are you gay or straight? Do you prefer meat or fish or are you vegetarian?

But if you ask *other* questions about individuals, you get very different results, for we are also social beings reflecting the time and place we were born and our experiences with others, particularly as children, even down to the most basic levels of who we are. Why is suicide more prevalent in some societies than others? Why are marriages more egalitarian in some societies than others? Marriage and suicide are individual choices, yet they clearly are choices reflecting patterns that include and extend beyond individuals.

I think we can assume individuals are at least as complex as photons.

THE CENTRALITY OF EMPATHY

There is another glaring absence in Ayn Rand's concept of the ideal individual, one that also helps explain why her characters, memorable as they are, were so unlike real human beings and why genuine individuality was discouraged among her closest followers. That missing quality is empathy. "Self-interest" turns out to be a very interesting concept. It turns out that in the absence of the capacity for empathy, the ability to act in rational self-interest is also absent.

What is "self-interest"? Rand and the libertarian tradition generally take the "self" for granted. The self is contrasted to other selves, and these selves gain when they cooperate, and at least one loses when one coerces another. In Rand's formulation, coercing another person makes the coercing dependent on its victim, and so not truly autonomous. Even the coercing self is not really free. As is so often the case, a partial truth is confused with the whole story.

There is nothing new about the argument that men and women act in their own self-interest. If we go back to the time of David Hume and Adam Smith, many argued that in the end all human action is self-interested. As Hume described this point, no "passion is or can be disinterested . . . even unknown to ourselves, we seek only our own gratification while we appear the most deeply engaged in schemes for the liberty and happiness of mankind."[73]

However, both he and Adam Smith emphasized that such an egoistic analysis fails to describe our actual experience. For example, Smith observes that when we are pleased by observing or displeased by not observing something in others, "fellow-feeling with all the emotions of our own breast—both the pleasure and the pain—are always felt so instantaneously, and often upon such frivolous occasions, that it seems evident that neither of them can be derived from any such self-interested consideration."[74]

When we rigorously examine it, egoism defeats itself. To act in self-interest beyond the spur of the moment, we need to anticipate our future situation. To do this, we imaginatively project ourselves into our anticipated future circumstances, and on that basis choose a course of action we believe will lead to a desirable outcome. This hypothetical future self of ours does not yet exist. It is a projection of who we think we will be at some future time.

Our ability to project our imagination into anticipated circumstances arises from what Hume and Smith termed our *sympathetic* capabilities. By sympathy they refer to what we would call empathy today. We identify with another being. Regardless of what we call it, sympathy, empathy, or identification, this trait is not simply a passion or feeling. Hume emphasizes that "we must be assisted by relations of resemblance and contiguity in order to feel the sympathy in its full perfection."[75]

The effective power of sympathy (empathy) cannot be simply taken for granted. Smith observes that "Men, though naturally sympathetic, feel . . .

little for another, with whom they have no particular connection, in comparison of what they feel for themselves."[76] For empathy to develop, our intellect is needed to grasp or deny relevant similarities. Our predisposition to empathy can be cultivated and strengthened, or it can be inhibited.

The *same* capacities, which enable us to put ourselves into our own future shoes, also enable us to put ourselves into the shoes of another. In both cases we project our present self into the imagined mind of another self. Rational self-interest, which depends upon being able to anticipate the probable future consequences arising for us from something we do now, requires that we have the same capacity to sympathize with others. In both cases the capacity depends on our ability to recognize similarities in beings other than our immediate self.[77] As we put ourselves in others' minds, based on their similarities with our own, we *care* about them.

Self-consciousness along with reason creates the capacity to care for others. Were we unaware of ourselves, we would have no basis for understanding a mind. Without reason we would have no basis for understanding experiences other than our own at the time we have the experience. *The greater our sense of self as a being extending over time, the greater becomes our capacity to empathize with other beings.* This is because the farther into the future our self-interest extends, the more developed our capacity for empathy must become, since our present situation, and the temptations and pains it presents, is ever farther removed from that imagined being for whom we can effectively care.

The more a being seems to resemble ourselves, the more easily we can empathize with it. Because we believe our own self is largely unchanging, when pursuing our rational self-interest, we usually extrapolate our present self into our future. When the future arrives we often discover we were wrong. We will often be closer to the mark in our empathy for a close friend today than for our imagined self ten years hence.

Sympathy (empathy), Hume observed, "extends itself beyond our own species."[78] Some species are more like ourselves than others. We can more easily sympathize with chimpanzees than with fish and fish more easily than with earthworms. But it is not the case that sympathy, even toward earthworms, is impossible. We have a gradation of similarities, and there-fore a gradation of the possibilities for sympathy, which never fall to zero. Even the simplest forms of life can flourish or fail, react to stimuli that are harmful or beneficial, and enjoy good or suffer ill health.[79]

An observation by Aldo Leopold helps us better appreciate these impli-cations of empathy. Leopold wrote that while we can mourn the demise of the passenger pigeon, which none of us has ever seen, no passenger pigeon would have mourned our own passing. He concluded, "For one species to mourn the death of another is a new thing under the sun."[80]

All life is related. The more closely the physical nervous system of an animal approaches our own, the stronger the burden of proof must be on those who say its experience is wholly unlike our own. It makes far more sense to say that we have important similarities with other forms of life than to wall our experience off from everything else in the world. Descartes could attempt this latter move because he believed in a tradi-tional, literal way in the Biblical book of Genesis, and allowed "doubt" to overwhelm common sense. But what excuse does a post-Darwinian have?

Once we admit to sharing significant traits with chimpanzees, we enter on to a continuum extending indefinitely far. The implications of this point were not lost on Charles Darwin, who wrote, "I have all my life been a strong advocate for humanity to animals, and have done what I could in my writings to enforce this duty."[81] Darwin believed that ultimately ethics would evolve to include all sentient beings, gradually expanding its scope as people came to see their similarities with ever more distant forms of life.[82] Like Hume and Smith, Darwin believed natural sympathy provided the *foundation* of moral action. On this basis, the theory of evolution expanded moral consideration to encompass all life, for we can no longer hold ourselves as truly separate from others.

Here is a contrasting definition as to what is valuable about human beings. Hume and Smith's analysis of sympathy explains why people would want to act ethically not through self-sacrifice, but through an ever-richer experience of self. We are not qualitatively unique among living species in rationality (crows, chimpanzees, and even fish and mollusks make tools to accomplish intended ends). We are, as Leopold observed, unique in our capacity to care for other beings of no utility to us and whom we have never seen. This capacity has nothing to do with self-interest the way Rand and libertarians in general define it, and requires instead the existence of a self that can grow to embrace ever more of the world. Empathy inclines us to wish well-being on at least all not actively injuring us.

GROUPS: "I AM BECAUSE WE ARE"

If individuals are more complex than atoms, groups are more complex than simple threats to individual freedom or collections of individuals pursuing mutually advantageous trade, as in the libertarian outlook. Relationships always occur in the context of groups. Since there cannot be individuals without relationships, so there cannot be individuals without groups

Initially a libertarian might reply, "But the real issue is whether or not the groups are voluntary." This is not true.

Beginning with our families, we are born into and live within groups we do not choose. For better or worse our parents' job of loving and raising us powerfully influences our beliefs, emotional security, self-image, tendency toward anger or love, and other dimensions in a list that goes on and on. If our families are wealthy, greater opportunities open up than if they are poor. On the other hand, too sheltered an upbringing can render us a kind of hothouse plant feeling at great risk if ever placed outside. We do not choose our families and for most of us our families are where we first learn about reality. They influence us at levels far deeper than where we make deliberate choices, at least without benefiting from input by friends or therapists who see patterns in our behavior we cannot.

The society we are born into is another group we do not choose. It also powerfully influences our life possibilities. It provides us with our initial language, customs, awareness of our place in the world, and much more. For Ayn Rand, once the Russian Revolution ended Tsarist discrimination against women and Jews, she could attend a university. When the

Bolsheviks began discriminating against the children of the "bourgeoi-sie," she was forced out. Both events powerfully influenced her subsequent career and outlook on life.

Many a banker or venture capitalist would live a far different life in a different society. Some of these people would die young if they were born into an overpopulated agricultural society. Others might become mediocre farmers or respected village headmen. The manipulative skills of a hedge fund billionaire would be of little value in most societies. Yet none of these people chose their place of birth, nor did they do anything to earn their initial place in the society in which they were born. Similarly, poor children did nothing to "earn" their place living with parents just scraping by.

Even after they attained adulthood and set off on their own, people attained success in most cases not simply through their unique abilities, real as they may be. First, they benefited from a social inheritance going back hundreds and even thousands of years, an inheritance they were lucky enough to acquire. Second, they lived in an environment where they had the good fortune to meet the right people at the right time, people who recognized their qualities and were in a position to reward them. Rand's immigration to the U.S. was made possible by loans from relatives already in America. People she subsequently met provided her crucial help at crucial times.

Of course hard work is also important especially for those not born to wealth, but many poor Mexican laborers work far harder than many Americans who are comparatively wealthy. Many people who rose from poverty to wealth worked hard, but many people work hard who do not rise from poverty to wealth. Creativity can also play a role in economic success, but creativity, even when honored long after the creator's death, is often not rewarded. Vincent Van Gogh's paintings have made millions of dollars for people who collected his work, but he himself lived and died in poverty. To make their millions all they did was recognize Van Gogh's work as worth more than the pittance he charged for it, or perhaps they simply acted from charity. A similar charitable act to another artist would have led to no fortune.

Along with individual ability and the environment into which they were born, luck is a vital part of economic success, especially big success. First there is the luck of being born in the right society at the right time, and then there is the luck involved in meeting the right people. The wisest free market thinkers are very clear about this. Nobel Laureate F. A. Hayek emphasized, "The element of luck is as inseparable from the operation of the market as the element of skill."[83] Luck and undeserved good fortune count for a lot in enabling material success in a market society. The market does NOT simply reward hard work and creativity. Again, think of Vincent Van Gogh.

COLLECTIVISM, INDIVIDUALS, AND GROUPS

A libertarian might respond that I am advocating "collectivism." Libertarians continually contrast individualism to collectivism. This was a major theme in Ayn Rand's work and is present in the work of nearly all other libertarians I have read. There is an important historical basis for this. Libertarianism's seminal thinkers lived during the time when communism seemed to many people a viable political and economic system, and when fascism, a collectivism on the right, had only been defeated through a long and bloody war. As an alternative to free societies, collectivism burned its image deeply into the consciousness of many who lived during this time.

Libertarian thinkers such as von Mises and F. A. Hayek were among the most powerful intellectual opponents of collectivist views. And ultimately their arguments prevailed just as collectivist societies proved less prosperous, less sustainable, and immeasurably more vicious than Western liberal democratic ones. Had von Mises and Hayek been better understood, many idealists would not have wasted their lives counting on communism to bring humanity a better life. Today, communism is gone and collectivism has few explicit defenders except for the excesses of virulent nationalism and the perpetual scourges of racism and theocracy.

The problem is that like victorious generals, victorious thinkers always seem prepared to wage the last war and never notice when their priorities and outlooks depart from new challenges. They see collectivism everywhere even when it isn't present. They view the present through the patterns they discerned in the past. Of course we all do this to some extent, but creative and perceptive minds are aware that these patterns change as the world changes. For the most part, libertarians today remain mired in intellectual outlooks rooted in the problems people faced during the 1930s and 40s.

SO WHAT IS COLLECTIVISM?

Collectivism is a modern form of tribalism, writ big. The idea behind collectivism is that there is one group so important, so decisive in determining who we are, that both our individuality and everything else fades into relative unimportance. Some on the left said this was true for economic classes. Some on the right claim it is true for races. Others make a similar claim on behalf of their religion. Perhaps the most effective collectivists have claimed as much for the nation or "the people." In all of these cases individual rights wither away when they stand in opposition to whatever group is regarded as all important.

Great crimes have been committed in the name of different collectivist identities, both internally and between different countries. Because collectivists have never agreed on which group is all-important, many wars have occurred between different collectivist nations. Nazi Germany's attack on Communist Russia is the bloodiest example. But collectivism has *nothing* to do with the argument that individuals are inextricably immersed in society.

There is no single-most-basic group. In practice we belong to many different groups, including culture, family, nation, economic class, race, gender, generation, religion, and on and on and on, down to our most subtle identifications with even transitory groups of friends and brief acquaintances. Some groups we belong to by choice, some by fate, and in our individuality we create a unique self that stands in both support and tension with all these various groups because we cannot be reduced to any one of them. Even if you and I belong to the same groups, the worlds we create will be different. But this hardly means groups are secondary to individuals. Groups are as constitutive of our individuality as individuals are constitutive of groups.

Because individuals can never be separated from groups and many are attached to us by fate not choice, the real issue is not simply keeping groups "voluntary," but rather *what are the most appropriate relations between an individual and a group?* Often they are simply voluntary, as when we join a club or a church. But in other contexts, the issue is that you are a member whether you want to be or not. What kinds of influence should you have in the group? And what kinds of influence should the group have on you?

A NEW COLLECTIVISM

Collectivism is the exaltation of a group and its well-being over the moral status of any individual within or without the group. Individuals can be sacrificed for the benefit of the group. Once we understand both what collectivism is *and* the failure of Rothbard and other economistic libertarians to grasp the tension between individuals and markets, we come to a disturbing insight. Much libertarian thought leads to a new collectivism. It is not intended to do so, but we know how the road to Hell is paved.

I explained above that as the market shifts from being dominated by individuals and family producers toward becoming ever more thoroughly comprised of corporations, the range of free choices within which individuals have to act gets more constrained. Prices shift from being signals indicating how individuals can make informed choices about means to their ends to becoming commands which, if not followed, will lead to their progressive elimination. A new group, one that responds only to a small fraction of what we regard as human values, has become a major arbiter of human fate, one that is limited only by people's capacity to not be subjected to corporate logic. In a sense it is not even a human group.

For all their talk about the sanctity of an individual, libertarians do not know what an individual is and so cannot really appreciate what is necessary to preserve individual freedom. Not knowing this, they also misunderstand their own nonaggression principle.

NONAGGRESSION AND PROPERTY

Using physical violence or its threat against another person is a pretty clear example of aggression. This image makes the libertarian nonaggression principle persuasive. But once we understand that individuals only exist within a context of relationships, other kinds of aggression become possible, the kinds libertarians cannot see. They believe we are distinct from our relationships and ultimately autonomous from them. Our experiences *happen* to the self rather than helping to constitute it.

This blindness plays out in a fascinating way when we examine the core libertarian concept of property. Libertarians claim that taking property against our will constitutes theft or robbery. Because they are not voluntary, taxes are a reason for their hatred of government. However, this reason is incoherent.

Where did *property* come from? Why is it legitimate for me to own something and only allow others to use it with my permission? The classic libertarian explanation is some variation of John Locke's argument that something unowned becomes ours when we "mix" our labor with it. Locke's initial example was picking up an acorn or apple to eat. This description seems reasonable, for hardly anyone would doubt that if I picked up an apple or acorn, it would make it mine.[84]

Owning an acorn or apple is reasonably derived from a Lockean argument because they have boundaries that for most purposes are clear to everyone. But for the most part, our world is not made up of neat bundles forming discrete units we can appropriate and exchange as our property. Further, if it is to be useful in a market economy, we must all agree as to what constitutes a unit of "property." Otherwise we cannot agree on what it is we are exchanging. Property rights need to be respected by all concerned.

Agreement about what constitutes property is necessary because without it there can be no market economy. But how do we reach this agreement? We cannot "let the market decide" because without defined property there cannot be a market to decide anything. Both historically and logically, property exists *prior* to the market.

So long as we consider property a "thing," using the acorn or apple as our universal example, we cannot answer our question. There are too many possible ways to define property. We encounter another version of the dilemma libertarians are impaled on, we see that they treat individuals as isolated units that can cooperate together, or not, depending on how they choose. Property is not an isolated thing existing distinct from the world in which it is found. *Property is a locus of rights to enter into relationships,* both with what is owned and with others.

There are two steps in attaining a better understanding of property.

First, think about what it means to own a house. In most cases I have complete control over it. I can remodel it, tear it down, live in it, let it stand vacant, or rent it out. Let's assume I decide to rent it out. I still own my house but I sell the right to its exclusive temporary use to another person so long as a mutually agreeable rent is paid. In doing so, I lose the right to enter my house whenever I want, whereas the renter, a non-owner, now has this right. But I still have other rights to the house, including raising the rent, selling it, remodeling it, or moving the renter out and moving in myself. This example leads to our first clarification about "property:" property is not a thing; it is a *bundle* of rights to be employed in certain ways if the owner so chooses. The owner can rent out some of the rights in that bundle and still retain the others.

Another example expands this point. Many land trusts preserve open space by encouraging property owners to sell their development rights to the trust, which has no intention of developing the property. The landowner still lives there and cannot be forced out by the owner of the development rights. The owner can still sell or bequeath the land, minus its development rights. He or she still has "private property," but the bundle of rights his ownership includes is smaller now.

The land trust example demonstrates that not only can some of the rights in a "bundle" be temporarily rented or leased, some can also be sold while the others remain under separate ownership by the original seller. To own property is to own rights to enter into relationships, not to own a thing, for neither the rancher nor the trust own "the land." This observation leads us to a second clarification in how we normally think about "property."

Bundles of property rights vary with the property. I can chop up my chair into kindling any time I want. In most societies I cannot chop up my living dog or cat any time I want. No one thinks it wrong to chop up a chair, but all normal people think it is wrong to chop up a living pet. I can sell someone the right to chop up my chair. I cannot sell someone the right to chop up my pet. Yet I still own my pet.

Consider a much less extreme example. In most cities I can play my music louder during the day than I can at night. Why? Because making noise is more appropriate during the day than late at night. Different times of day determine different contents to my bundle of rights to use my drums. As a physical object my drums remain the same, but considered as my property, the rights in my bundle vary over time and in relationship to others. In normal societies, no one finds this at all strange.

Bundles of discrete property rights vary with what is considered an *appropriate relation* with the property and its environment. What is appropriate differs with regard to chairs and to cats and to music. They also vary depending on what are considered appropriate relations with others such as my neighbors. We are back to that concept so irritating for libertarians: relationships. The "thingness" of property manifests in being the physical referent for our bundle of rights that give us some sphere of control over it. But the rights in that bundle are defined in terms of appropriate relationships into which I can enter with and through my property. Property therefore implies a concept of what constitutes appropriate relations both with what is owned and with others.

From this perspective a world of private property is a world where a wide number of cooperative relationships can be entered into with others, depending only on mutual agreement. So far Ayn Rand and other libertarians might remain happy, if uneasy with the unaccustomed terminology. But their smiles fade when we ask the next question.

WHO DECIDES?

Who determines what relationships involving property are appropriate? Let's return to the issue of noise. In terms of either its volume or the time of day, there is no clear point identifying when we should shift from the greater permissiveness for loud noises during the day to the greater restrictions of night. Yet somehow a point and volume must be determined, and normally it must apply equally to everyone within a given area.

Traditionally, a libertarian will say property is misused when someone's boundary is involuntarily crossed. That constitutes aggression. At first this standard sounds reasonable and as usual, it masks a deeper reality. Noise *always* crosses boundaries and no one would argue that all noise should be eliminated unless it is expressly allowed by all who hear it. That would be absurd. The same point holds for auto exhaust, barbeque smoke, cigarette smoke, bright light, and many other things. We are immersed in relationships where acts by others cross our boundaries without our permission and we do the same in return, and it is obviously ridiculous to call all such phenomena aggression.

It is equally absurd to say that no such boundary crossings are inappropriate. Some easily can be considered aggression. Very few libertarians, and no sane ones, would say setting firecrackers off in my back yard at 3 a.m. just to wake you up is not some kind of aggression. Yet based on their principles, libertarians cannot answer how to make such a determination. At what point can you legitimately shift from wearing earplugs and running a white noise machine to calling the cops?

Libertarian theorist Murray Rothbard once argued that no one should be able to pollute another person without his or her consent. From this perspective no one was "greener" than Rothbard on pollution. Then someone pointed out to him that if that were the case no one could run an internal combustion engine without the consent of all who could breathe its fumes, at least if they found it interfered with their enjoyment of their property. Rothbard then went from too stringent a standard to effectively none at all, arguing the individual polluter had to be identified so he or she could be held personally responsible. "The guilty polluter should be each individual car owner and not the automobile manufacturer, who is not responsible for the actual tort and the actual emission."[85]

As a practical matter that is often impossible. Rothbard did suggest that in a pure "stateless" libertarian society the roads would be privately owned and the owner of the road could then be held liable for pollution. But even a moment's thought demonstrates the absurdity of his argument.

Think of Beijing and the smog it produces, smog that mixes pollution from cars and industry. This smog kills people. A comprehensive study of the health and economic costs of smog in the Los Angeles basin and California's San Joaquin Valley concluded that attaining the ideal federal standard for clean air "would save more lives than reducing the number of motor vehicle fatalities to zero in most of the counties in this study."[86] People could be dropping dead from poisoned air within a Rothbardian society without having any legal resource so long as enough separate sources contributed to the poison. No one could now be browner than Rothbard.

Advocating these ridiculous extremes arises because treating property as a thing with objective boundaries misidentifies it. Property always exists in and through relationships. Some relationships are legitimate, some are illegitimate, and in some cases a line must be drawn that could be drawn in many possible places. Libertarianism has nothing to offer us as guidance in such important cases. It cannot even understand the problem.

There is still another complication in determining what constitutes appropriate property rights, and pollution helps us see it clearly. Many cities develop serious air pollution when they grow large enough that practices once entirely harmless begin to adversely impact more and more people, beginning with those who are the most sensitive. In other words, not only can responsibility for pollution not be laid at the foot of individual polluters, in time what was once not pollution can become pollution.

Missoula, Montana, had to face an air quality problem when its population growth plus normal air inversions during the winter trapped increasingly dangerous quantities of wood smoke in the air. What was once entirely acceptable for everyone became lethal for increasing numbers of people unless something was done. What was once clearly an allowable right might become a prohibited use at another, meaning that one right in a bundle—heating my home by enjoying a wintertime fire in my fireplace—might be removed from it.

Who decides what the allowable boundaries will be? Who decides when conditions have changed? Ayn Rand's vision of completely independent people owning discrete properties and contracting with one another over them is only a part of human reality, and as we become ever more numerous and interconnected, it becomes increasingly misleading when considered by itself. But how can change or lack of change be justified to those with different ideas as to what should be done?

Things bleed out into the world and interpenetrate at least through some combination of sound, photons, and smell. We need to come to agreement about how much of this bleeding out is acceptable and what is beyond the pale. I cannot detonate firecrackers in my neighborhood at 3 a.m., but I can talk with a friend on the sidewalk at that time. Both create noise that might disturb someone. I can have an outdoor light by my front door and leave it on all night, but I cannot buy a searchlight and aim it at your bedroom window. Both examples create photons that cross your property boundaries. Where between these extremes do we draw the line?

There are *no* clear lines between acceptable and unacceptable pollution by chemicals, noise, odors, or light, yet we need to have one if we are to have a system where contractual agreements work for the ultimate benefit of all and where no one is aggressed upon. This is true even if all we want are useful engines and breathable air. An atomistic view of property *cannot* solve this problem, either.

The only way to define rights when people disagree so that the inevitable losers will recognize the outcome as legitimate is to be fair to all sides, *and the only way to be considered fair is if everyone affected by the decision gets some opportunity for equal input into the decision.* If you have more input than me at every point, and my view fails to make a difference while yours prevails, I will reasonably regard the outcome as unfair. I will rightfully feel coerced. *Absent fairness over these decisions, even the seriously inadequate libertarian view of the nonaggression principle is violated.*

Property rights cannot be derived without some prior collective means for making decisions. Further, these rights will need a way to be changed from time to time should the need arise, as with our examples of air pollution in Missoula. Deciding when the need arises should also be done fairly. Because boundaries are never completely clear, different people can and most certainly will sincerely disagree on where they should be drawn. A principle of fairness in determining property rights is necessary for any kind of nonaggression principle to be honored. Only when they believe they have lost their case fairly will losers accept a decision as legitimately decided even when they disagree with it. *Yet libertarians have no such principle.* They first assume property and then worry about coercion. In the most basic sense, this position is incoherent.

UNDERSTANDING DEMOCRACY

By uncovering what has been assumed regarding the most basic concepts in most libertarian theorizing, we have arrived at several insights. First, far from being independent of society, individuals are only comprehensible as members of society, and in any *human* sense are impossible in its absence. Second, the property rights libertarians rightly identify as necessary for individuals to exercise freedom are socially determined and must exist prior to the market. Third, those rights can often be delineated along different lines, none more objectively real or just than another. Consequently, if decisions about property rights are to be made without aggression, the rules leading to those decisions must be perceived as fair to all sides. Fourth, for boundaries and rules to be fair, they must treat everyone equally. Given the nonaggression principle libertarians say they hold dear, some kind of democracy is the unavoidable result.

We can see this issue clearly by examining a controversy arising from the contemporary libertarian strategy to dominate New Hampshire. Because New Hampshire is a small state, many libertarians have moved there in hopes of eventually controlling its politics. The results have been interesting.

A libertarian activist was recently sentenced to 100 days in jail for refusing to remove a couch from his back yard in Keene, New Hampshire, and for a series of problems that escalated from his response to the initial charges.[87] Libertarians see him as a victim of "tyranny." Whether or not the fellow is getting treated fairly, there is another issue to explore: the right of democratic government to regulate how property is used.

From a libertarian perspective, why is Keene in the wrong? Let's consider another example to help clarify the issue. For libertarians, a homeowners' association can legitimately make similar rules about what is and is not acceptable outside a member's home. I know outdoor clotheslines are often not acceptable in such associations, so it is easy to imagine them also not accepting a couch. From a libertarian standpoint they are in the right. So why would libertarians think that the town of Keene is in the wrong?

Usually, libertarians answer that the two cases are different because the association is contractually based and no one had to buy a home there, whereas Keene has a town government making decisions for its approximately 23,400 citizens. For them, the problem is that Keene is a democratic town.

There are two devastating answers to this argument. First, and least penetrating, libertarians have chosen to move to New Hampshire and to Keene. They did not have to do so. But, having done so, they voluntarily accepted its decisions over property use as much as if Keene had been a homeowners' association. I think this is a good response, but some libertarians will argue that governments have monopolized all land so they have no choice but to live somewhere. The next response is more fatal to their argument.

If the principle of nonaggression is to be honored, democratic procedures are the only way decisions can be made when establishing a community's basic framework of property rights. Further, it must be able to alter those bundles when the community deems it necessary, as in Missoula. The contractual homeowners' association is itself dependent upon there first being democratic decision-making to decide what rights should accompany ownership of private property. Only then can property owners form an association.

The hypothetical homeowners' association as well as Keene's town council objected to couches because they could be seen off the property. Photons depicting these objects crossed boundaries and invaded the vision of un-consenting others. There is no objective line to determine when a photonic trespass has occurred and when it has not. Some will think couches qualify, others will disagree. The issue must therefore be determined by some decision-making authority, be it governmental or contractual. Whatever the decision, it remains a matter of human judgment.

I have already argued that short of a decision-making process that treats all involved in the issue equally, even with a narrow libertarian interpretation of aggression, there is no non-aggressive means for making the decision. Therefore, a democratic body has the right to make the decisions Keene's town government made. Keene's government may not have acted wisely in making the ordinance, but it certainly acted legitimately.

Keene's decision could be criticized by libertarians on two other grounds. First, perhaps the process was not democratic enough. It was not fair to all voters. Second, it was a mistake and should be revisited. Democratic principles provide a way to think clearly about both issues, whereas libertarian principles do not.

The first objection can easily be met by improving the democratic quality of Keene's government. Give all citizens a significant point where their views are treated equally. Make it *more democratic.*

The principle of democracy solves the second objection. Citizens unhappy with the initial decision can argue in public to change the council's mind and, failing that, run for election. If they have convinced a majority of residents that they are right and the issue is important, they will win and the incumbents be ousted. Perhaps under current circumstances, reforms need to be made to better enable these processes to take place, but that is arguing while accepting the legitimacy of democracy. Libertarians cannot coherently criticize Keene's decision as illegitimate just because a democratic government made it.

DEMOCRACY AND GAMES

Libertarians continually speak of democracies as "states," and states have a long history of being oppressive, violent, and corrupt. But this is a flawed framing of democratic reality.[88] We need a better framework, one that can separate the essential things a democracy must do if a society is to meet standards for nonaggression. This would be different from the issues of starting wars and killing dissidents that states have specialized in.

If this cannot be done, the nonaggression principle is itself radically flawed because we have seen that the democratic principle is essential for private property to justly exist. The principle of a state is sovereign power over subjects. States rule over people. The principle of democracy is self-government. Both states and democracies make rules, but different people with very different statuses in society make the rules and different standards justify them. If we refuse to distinguish between democracies and states because both make rules we may end up doing the equivalent of equating the moon with a grapefruit because both are round.

In important respects the democratic process is analogous to a game. Both democracies and games establish rules that strive to be free from bias, enabling us to determine fair winners in contests where incompatible goals are pursued. Only one side can win a game, and politics often has winners and losers. Importantly, in a game or in a democracy the ultimate loser plays by rules agreed upon in advance. At the outset no one knows who will win. The requirement for fair procedures is necessary because everyone knows they will not agree on all particular outcomes, yet decisions are still essential. No one would accord a heavier weight to another when by doing so they increase their likelihood of losing on future decisions of importance to them. It is easy to imagine a community of people who know that decisions will need to be made where they will sometimes disagree and who still *unanimously* adopt rules enabling these decisions to be made.

The claim that democratic government is "rule by a tyrannical majority" is *almost always* **absurd.** In almost every case it is akin to saying that the winners of a chess or baseball game have oppressed the losers. Bills of rights, regular elections, recalls, and similar measures are often agreed to unanimously in order to minimize cases where a temporary majority will establish rule over others while still enabling work to get done. The importance of these measures is clear when we reflect that during times when a powerful and monolithic majority exists, democracies act *most undemocratically.* The issue is fairness and equality, not majority rule.

Democracy is always a balancing act between the desirability of universal agreement and the reality of inevitable disagreement over decisions that must be made. It need not always lead to rules allowing a simple majority decision. Sometimes a "super majority," or greater than 50 percent majority, is preferred. Often, day-to-day affairs are decided by simple majorities, but changes in the basic rules (constitutional amendments) require decisions from supermajorities.

In *The Federalist Papers,* James Madison disposed of the libertarian argument against majority rule over 150 years before there were libertarians around to make it. The Constitution's advocates had been asked whether allowing majorities to pass laws might lead to abuses. Might supermajorities be better safeguards to our liberty? Madison replied,

> *That some advantages might have resulted from such a precaution cannot be denied . . . But these considerations are outweighed by . . . all cases where justice or the general good might require new laws to be passed, or active measures to be pursued . . . It would be no longer the majority that would rule: the power would be transferred to the minority.*[89]

In *Federalist 51*, Madison had already argued that by requiring agreement from the House, Senate, and Executive, the potential abuses of majority rule had been much reduced. Three majorities elected in three different ways would serve to protect the nation against partial factions with temporary majorities seeking their own advantage at everyone else's expense. The House was elected for short terms based on population. The Senate for longer terms, and staggered so it could never be replaced all at once. Senators were also elected by state. The president was elected by an electoral college that equaled the total of House and Senate members from each state. Though differently constituted, majorities in the United States have worked fairly well, with the exception of during the Civil War. At least, they worked until the rise of huge fortunes undercut the independence of all branches of government.

Today, all branches of government are subordinated to the power of great wealth protected by corrupt judicial rulings, as well as bought-and-paid-for politicians. Madison's warnings about blackmail and rule by minorities have been ignored, and we have repeatedly experienced the kind of damage small Senate minorities have done to our country by preventing even routine actions from being accomplished by majority vote. Again, libertarians have nothing of interest to say about these problems.

EQUALITY CANNOT BE SEPARATED
FROM FREEDOM

We can now see why the democratic principle of one-person-one-vote is central to a fair political process. It may not be enough, but it must be a part of the process. This principle helps establish fair procedures for discovering the rules applying to all of us. As part of a discovery process, neither this principle nor any other can guarantee success in any given instance. But no discovery process—be it in the market or science or anywhere else—can make this guarantee. That is why we call it a discovery process. That is why we seek fair rules for participating. We seek to discover what we do not know. In its absence we have only the oppression of the powerless for the benefit of the powerful, something libertarians claim they oppose.

Democracies exist primarily to discover and establish *public values*. A public value is a value people believe should apply within their society as a whole. It is different from a private value because its advocates the belief that it should apply more broadly than would be the case if left to the independent decisions of individuals. Of course, proposed public values can be contradictory, as with contemporary claims that gays should be able to marry and receive the legal privileges currently going to married couples, and that gay marriage should be constitutionally banned. Every society has public values, and what they are and how they might be changed is an issue within every community. But not every society has such values decided justly. *Finding, preserving, and modifying public values as determined by equal members of the community is the core of a democratic conception of politics.*

As an economy develops people are linked together with greater intensity into increasingly complex networks. New boundary issues continue to arise (no one wanted to put a muffler on a horse), and new rules must be made while others fall into disuse. This explains another contradiction between libertarian dogma and human reality.

There are many more limitations on some kinds of behavior in cities than in the countryside. Taxes are also higher. Yet for most people cities allow for a richer life with more choices than does the countryside. Living alone on a desert island is a libertarian utopia: complete self-sufficiency and no coercion at all. Yet, almost anyone would give up this freedom in order to live in even a poorly governed city. There is no correlation between the amount of liberty a person enjoys and governmentally enforced rules that limit some kinds of actions.

Ayn Rand herself famously chose to live as much of her life as she could in New York City. She had no interest in living in Bird City, Kansas, which is much more lightly regulated. Millions of Americans agree with her. Property values in New York and Bird City reflect people's contrasting desires to live in these places. A search for the real estate values in Bird

City reveal a three-bedroom, two-bath home is on the market there for just under 150 thousand dollars. In New York City, three-bedroom, two-bath homes start at just under two million dollars. A lot more people want to live in New York than in the "freer" environment of Bird City. For some reason, more businesses want to locate in New York as well. Are all these people simply passive subjects willing to live as slaves? Does this describe Ayn Rand, who because her income came from high royalty checks, could live anywhere in the U.S.?

Because libertarianism treats democracy as simply one more organized means by which some people coerce others, it has no way of solving the most basic issues that need addressing if a society based on nonaggression is to exist beyond the scale of a small tribe. Nor can it understand why most people, including libertarians, prefer more regulated large cities to the greater "freedom" of small rural communities, as their "dollar votes" abundantly and almost universally confirm.

BLINDNESS TO CONSEQUENCES: THE ISSUE OF RIGHT RELATIONSHIPS BETWEEN PEOPLE

Ron Paul is probably the best-known libertarian in America. When he stops speaking in broad generalities about why aggression is bad and gets into specifics, and when the individual-as-distinct side of who we are is most relevant, he is often insightful. On the other hand, when our relational side is more important, Paul's views are often deeply unjust, illuminating the practical and moral disasters justified by the libertarian misunderstanding of the nonaggression principle. For example, while critiquing the idea of enforceable employee rights Ron Paul said,

> *Employee rights are said to be valid when employers pressure employees into sexual activity. Why don't they quit once the so-called harassment starts? Obviously the morals of the harasser can't be defended, but how can the harassee escape some responsibility for the problem? Seeking protection under civil rights legislation is hardly acceptable.*[90]

There are many levels of theoretical and moral blindness in Paul's statement. These weaknesses are found in libertarian arguments in general.

Blindness 1: All Exchanges Are Not Equal

Paul writes as if finding jobs is as simple as deciding to buy a toothbrush. The market offers jobs as it offers toothbrushes and we pick the one we like most at a mutually agreeable price. Like toothbrushes, lots of choices are out there. If a boss is a jerk just get another one.

But for almost everyone, quitting a job to find another is neither easy nor pleasant. Needed income is abandoned in the hope of getting replacement income before savings run out. If the harassee supports a family, other people, often including children, are dependent on the income. To quit a job threatens their well-being. We also know what can happen when someone falls behind in paying a mortgage. A new job often requires a letter of recommendation from the old employer, and he can use that need to pressure his employees for sexual favors even if they are taking Ron Paul's advice. All of these issues can make it very risky and stressful for a person dissatisfied with current job conditions to seek another one. In all these instances, individuals' relationships with other individuals beyond just the boss are powerful influences in how they choose. This is not like buying a toothbrush.

As it happens even as I write this there is a very concrete illustration of my point happening within the libertarian community. CATO is the most prominent libertarian think tank in the United States. The Koch brothers, Charles and David, who helped start it many years ago, are now seeking to take it over completely. The Kochs have contributed nothing to the organization for years. CATO has survived and prospered on its own. The libertarians who now populate it are fighting back in the name of freedom of thought. One of them, Julian Sanchez, is threatening to quit if the Kochs prevail. Sanchez writes, "I'm in no great hurry to leave a job I enjoy a lot—so I'm glad this will probably take a while to play out either way. But since I'm relatively young, and unencumbered by responsibility for a mortgage or kids, I figure I may as well say up front that if the Kochs win this one, I will."[91] No better rebuttal to Ron Paul's complete inability to understand people different from himself could have been penned by a liberal. If Sanchez were older, with a family and mortgage, it would be much riskier for him to quit and innocent others could suffer greatly from his choice.

These issues are rendered invisible within the libertarians' impoverished understanding of what it is to be an individual. They cannot distinguish between deciding how much to pay for a toothbrush and getting and keeping a job. A framework that cannot see these differences, so important to us in our daily lives, is pretty useless as a guide to understanding human life.

Blindness 2: All Exchanges Are Not between Equals

But there is a still deeper blindness. In many economic texts, exchanges and contracts are described as purchasing "widgets." Widgets are left undefined, so that the student can pay attention to the pure logic of exchange. If something concrete is specified, it is usually akin to trading so much wheat for so many chickens. The text then announces that after the exchange both parties are better off than they were before the exchange. Libertarians inevitably emphasize this aspect of voluntary exchange: when both parties are formally free, all exchanges leave both better off than if they had not made the exchange.

But formal equality does not come close to comprehending the many differences possible in human contractual exchanges. Let's pause a moment to envision an exchange between people who are roughly equal. It would resemble the basic economics text example of me having more wheat than I can use and you having more chickens than you can use. By trading some chickens for some wheat, we are both better off. If our exchange does not happen, neither of us is made worse off. We just do not benefit as we could have had we been able to agree. In a fair exchange, both parties are also honest and have all relevant information about the other's item in order to evaluate the desirability of their offer. Under such circumstances, all voluntary exchanges will indeed leave both parties better off that they were before the transaction.

But, to the extent that these concretely equal conditions disappear, even while the parties' formal equality remains, a purely formal description becomes inadequate to understand the relations between them. The classic case is that you are lost in a desert and dying of thirst. I happen upon you and offer you water if you sign your house and car over to me. Your option is to die, and so you sign. We are both better off. You are continuing to live and I have acquired a house and a car in exchange for a gallon of water. But, is it an exchange between equals? No normal person would say it was. Formal equality can conceal a yawning inequality. No sane social order would countenance such a contract. In decent places property rights do not include that particular bundle, they do not honor that particular kind of relationship. Once this point is understood, the adequacy of formal equality as sufficient for judging all "voluntary" contractual exchanges falls apart.

Employer/employee relations are almost never equal ones. Usually, many workers are seeking a few jobs and so a few employers have their choice among many workers. For all too many people, exercising power over subordinates is enjoyable. Were it the other way around, working conditions would be very different. There would be next to no sexual harassment because either it would be very expensive to hire a replacement employee, or leaving would be easy. We see this happening today with movie and music stars and the best professional athletes. These examples of substantial employee power are rare and always will be, and they prove the rule.

Power indeed tends to corrupt, and unequal bargaining power in contracts tends to lead to corrupt contracts; the greater the inequality, the greater the tendency. The enormously wealthy David and Charles Koch have funded a great many of libertarianism's most visible organizations. They also defrauded an Indian tribe in a contract over an oil pipeline. Fortunately, the Indians had a reasonably honest government to which they could take their case. The Kochs were fined $200 million. Appalled by Charles' and David's dishonest methods, a younger brother, Bill Koch, agreed with the verdict, observing it "shows they are the biggest crooks in the oil industry."[92] Little guys are treated far more harshly than the powerful. Yet, libertarians claim government is the enemy of business. More democracy is the cure, not less.

Blindness 3: What Constitutes a Contract?

Property rights and relatively free markets arose within societies long dominated by rigid legal hierarchies between the privileged and the rest of us. This legal framework defined relations between "superior" and "subordinate." Many linguistic terms survive to remind us of this past; terms such as "boss," "my employee," "my man," "my subordinate," and so on. Those on top shaped how wage relations evolved to ensure they evolved in their favor. It is not immediately obvious how much authority a purchaser of another's labor gets over the employee, particularly rightful authority. The powerful want it to be everything.

I have heard slavery defended four times in my life. Once was by a drunk Southern Republican, but the other three times were by libertarians. Two of these defenses were made to my face; the other was in print, by the prominent libertarian philosopher Robert Nozick.[93] Except for the Republican, their reasoning always went along the same line: so long as one *voluntarily* sold oneself into slavery, no harm was done. They were blind to the circumstances that might lead someone to do that.

In *The Huffington Post* I read of Monique Zimmerman-Stein, who has a rare genetic eye disease that causes blindness if left untreated. Her daughters also have it. She has decided to forgo treatments that can preserve her sight so she can put those funds into saving her daughters' sight. The injections that might help cost 380 dollars after insurance, and she needs one every six weeks. If she sold herself into slavery (or perhaps prostitution) to achieve the same goal, she could probably save her vision as well. Her purchaser likely would not want a blind slave. I suspect more than a few libertarians would praise the "freedom" that made her choice possible.[94]

These libertarians were also blind to the corrupting influence that own-ing slaves would have on the person doing the buying, a point Thomas Jefferson had made long ago, and later echoed in Lord Acton's adage that "power tends to corrupt and absolute power corrupts absolutely." So obsessed were they by the delights of abstract theorizing that they did not oppose arbitrary despotic power of one person over another unless it was by "The State" or by a common criminal. That libertarianism can be so easily and not unfairly linked to such possibilities is a sad commentary on its inability to comprehend the value of freedom, despite its posturing to the contrary.

But there is worse still. Adopting a theory that elevates abstract con-tract above concrete human beings made it impossible to understand our own founding document. The Declaration of Independence spoke of "inalienable" rights not as a rhetorical flourish, but to make the point that slavery could never be legitimate under any circumstances. A person could not give another responsibility for their life choices and the use they made of their freedom. There were some things that one simply could not do, even if all involved acted in some sense voluntarily.[95] Libertarians too often honor contract over people. As they do, they also honor the arbi-trary authority of concrete people over other, weaker people and call it freedom. George Orwell would understand.

In 1911 at the Triangle Shirtwaist Factory, seamstresses were locked in to the factory so they could not leave until the workday ended.[96] The building caught fire and 146 girls and women, most between 16 and 23 years old, died horrible deaths. The fire escape was inadequate and col-lapsed. There were only twenty-seven buckets of water to put out the fire. The owners were not convicted of manslaughter, as they should have been. They did ultimately lose a civil suit in which plaintiffs won 75 dol-lars compensation per deceased victim. The company's insurance paid the owners about 400 dollars per casualty. One owner was later arrested for again locking the exit to his factory during working hours. He was fined twenty dollars. Except for the fine, this outcome, involving as it did insur-ance companies and financial recompense, seems in perfect keeping with libertarian principles, but hardly with humane or even minimally decent ones.

This kind of abuse of employer power was only effectively pushed back against with the rise of unions and the regulations Ron Paul and other libertarians denounce as diminishing their "freedom." Today, among the bundle of rights an employer purchases when hiring labor, imprisoning workers during working hours is not included. Today, in large part through libertarian influence, there is a move to return to the good old days of 1911. The laws of contract that are so equal when viewed abstractly can be lethally unequal when actually applied to human beings in the complexity of life as it is really lived.

These problems are rendered *invisible* with the libertarians' very selective interpretation of the non-coercion principle. After all, they might say, those dead employees had the option of quitting. They did not have to agree to the contract.

Blindness 4: Immorality in the Name of Morality

In the passage from Ron Paul quoted above, he refers to "so-called" sexual harassment. In Paul's statement he admits that the harasser is morally wrong, but the harassment is "so-called." This is very strange. The only way I can see any coherence at all in it is to assume that, in Paul's view, harassing a subordinate for sexual favors counts as being rude, undesirable, and nothing more. Apparently, this is because the harasser did not threaten physical violence if he did not get his way. Paul simply cannot recognize power that cannot easily be reduced to the use or threat of physical violence. As such, he can neither condemn the immorality of those who abuse many kinds of power, nor can he truly appreciate the situations of those subjected to it.

This is a clear example of what I regard as the chief moral weakness of many libertarians. They appear unable to imaginatively place themselves in the shoes of people unlike themselves. They have a failure in empathy. Paul, a very well-to-do doctor, can easily end connections with annoying or abusive people, so apparently for him, anyone can. Ron Paul has power a waitress or a maid does not, ironically power made all the stronger because of his government-protected privileges as a licensed physician. This power prevents him from appreciating what it is like to be relatively powerless.

The failure to recognize the importance of empathy in what makes us human spills over in a failure to recognize the true richness of human relationships in the world. Caught in a kind of theoretical autism, libertarians fall back on abstractions incapable of appreciating basic moral principles. In the process they end up being blind to immorality.

Blindness to Possibilities

When people have blinded themselves to concrete problems due to abstract reasoning, they also blind themselves to possible solutions to those problems, even solutions in harmony with their abstract reasoning. I will give one example, but there are many. We have established that there is a genuine problem in libertarians' failure to recognize the reality of concrete power differences between people who are abstractly equal. We have also established that this theoretical assumption on their part is arbitrary and guarantees their failure to understand their own nonaggression principle.

Ironically, their nonaggression principle combined with free contract and a market economy can effectively address these issues. And it has already done so spectacularly for more than fifty years. But libertarians have been completely uninterested in these developments, all the while arguing for greater arbitrary power on behalf of employers.

Consider for example the Mondragón Cooperatives in Spain. They are worker-owned, market based, contractual, and voluntary. They lack the hierarchical and often abusive relationships that forced workers to organize unions in self-defense in the United States and elsewhere. They are also quite profitable and have thrived and expanded for more than fifty years.

The Mondragón Cooperatives have solved or substantially improved upon many of the problems that libertarians are blind to seeing. They have also been a major factor in turning one of Spain's poorest regions into one of its most prosperous, with an unusually low unemployment rate. Further, they have done so within a framework that does not violate libertarian principles! Yet to my knowledge, not a single libertarian has given them any informed attention. The most recent study of the Mondragón Cooperatives is by socialist Carl Davidson. That Davidson can define as socialism what is completely in harmony with libertarian principles is ironic evidence of libertarians being unable to comprehend their own principles and their inability to appreciate what constitutes human beings as individuals.[97]

This glaring absence of interest illustrates a breathtaking lack of awareness of the possibilities that can be achieved within the context of voluntary contract and freedom, values libertarians believe in. I suspect this is because the issue of relationships is invisible to them beyond the obvious case of whether or not I point a gun at you. *Their defective understanding of their own principles has caused them to miss some of the most exciting examples of wonderful and sustainable innovations growing from those same principles of respecting individuals, contractual property rights, and the nonaggression principle.*

RETURNING TO RAND

As I bring this discussion to a close I wish to return to Ayn Rand. I have shown that the Rothbardian and Friedmanite versions of libertarianism cannot protect individual freedom. But Rand has always been billed as an absolute defender of individual rights. Many passages in Rand's work seem to support the view that she takes rights as absolute, as in *The Virtue of Selfishness*, where she writes:

> *When one speaks of man's right to exist for his own sake, for his own rational self-interest, most people assume automatically that this means his right to sacrifice others. Such an assumption is a confession of their own belief that to injure, enslave, rob or murder others is in man's self-interest—which he must selflessly renounce. The idea that man's self-interest*

*can be served only by a non-sacrificial relationship with others has never
occurred to those humanitarian apostles of unselfishness, who proclaim
their desire to achieve the brotherhood of men. And it will not occur to
them, or to anyone, so long as the concept "rational" is omitted from the
context of "values," "desires," "self-interest" and "ethics."*[98]

This statement would seem to make Rand a powerful advocate for
inalienable rights to individual freedom from coercion by others. Might
she be immune to the kinds of criticisms I have given of Rothbard and
Friedman? Consider this passage.

THE QUESTION OF AMERICAN INDIANS

During her 1974 address at West Point, when a Native American cadet
asked her what she thought of earlier aggression against American Indians, Rand said:

*They had no right to a country merely because they were born here
and then acted like savages. The white man did not conquer this country. And you're a racist if you object, because it means you believe
that certain men are entitled to something because of their race. You
believe that if someone is born in a magnificent country and doesn't
know what to do with it, he still has a property right to it. He does
not. Since the Indians did not have the concept of property or property rights—they didn't have a settled society, they had predominantly
nomadic tribal "cultures"—they didn't have rights to the land, and
there was no reason for anyone to grant them rights that they had not
conceived of and were not using. It's wrong to attack a country that
respects (or even tries to respect) individual rights. If you do, you're an
aggressor and are morally wrong. But if a "country" does not protect
rights—if a group of tribesmen are the slaves of their tribal chief—why
should you respect the "rights" that they don't have or respect? The
same is true for a dictatorship. The citizens in it have individual rights,*

but the country has no rights and so anyone has the right to invade it, because rights are not recognized in that country; and no individual or country can have its cake and eat it too—that is, you can't claim one should respect the "rights" of Indians, when they had no concept of rights and no respect for rights. But let's suppose they were all beautifully innocent savage—which they certainly were not. What were they fighting for, in opposing the white man on this continent? For their wish to continue a primitive existence; for their "right" to keep part of the earth untouched—to keep everybody out so they could live like animals or cavemen. Any European who brought with him an element of civilization had the right to take over this continent, and it's great that some of them did. The racist Indians today—those who condemn America—do not respect individual rights.[99]

These sentiments were not a minor part of her thinking. They were republished in 2005 in *Ayn Rand Answers: The Best of Her Q & A.*

When push came to shove Rand rejected universal rights. Some people deserve rights and others do not, based on choices they have made regarding the lives they live. Indians made the wrong choices. Rand in the most literal sense did not know what she was talking about regarding Indians, but her error was deeper than ignorance. As with those who reduce human freedom to the market, Rand ultimately had no understanding of human rights.

FACTUAL ERRORS

A great many Indian tribes were in fact agricultural, and private property in resources was hardly unknown among them.[100] Even among hunting tribes, families sometimes owned specific territories or favored positions along a river. The land Europeans thought was unmodified had in fact often been extensively modified by Indians for thousands of years. Even now the extent and genius of those modifications is still being discovered, as with the recent uncovering of the human origins for good topsoil in the Amazon and the importance of biochar in building up good soil.

Far from living "like animals or cavemen," many of the world's most important crops were first domesticated by Indians. A partial list includes corn, squash, tomatoes, potatoes, chocolate, peppers, avocados, blueberries, cranberries, pineapples, peanuts, and many varieties of beans, quinoa, pecans, and turkeys. Imagine Italian food without tomatoes, Irish food without potatoes, Valentine's Day without chocolate, or Halloween without pumpkins.

Indians also often treated one another better than did the European colonists of the time. Missionaries were often shocked (and disturbed) at the respect Indians showed women compared to how Europeans acted. In the Mohawk Confederacy, the most powerful Northeastern tribe, women exercised considerable political power, while they were completely excluded from doing so by Europeans. In no tribe of my knowledge was there anything remotely like tribal members being "slaves of their tribal chiefs," a view more closely resembling European arguments defending absolute monarchy.

There were hundreds of different tribes from hunter-gatherers in the subarctic, where agriculture was impossible to cities, sometimes large ones, surrounded by farmland in the southern U.S. and Meso and South America. Some were brutal empires ultimately replaced by brutal European empires, as the Aztecs were by Spain. Others were societies so free and open that European colonies had to pass laws forbidding their members from leaving to join the neighboring Indians. In reality, thousands of Europeans voluntarily joined neighboring tribes, whereas so far as I know, no Indians voluntarily joined Europeans, a fact much commented on at the time. As with the Communists outlawing immigration to the West, English colonies finally had to outlaw Europeans joining the Indians.

In a careful study of America's early "white Indians," James Axtell concludes,

> *The great majority of white Indians left no explanations for their choice. Forgetting their original language and their past, they simply disappeared into their adopted society. But those captives who*

returned to write narratives of their experiences left several clues to
the motives of those who chose to stay behind. They stayed because
they found Indian life to possess a strong sense of community, abun-
dant love, and un-common integrity—values that the English colo-
nists also honored, if less successfully. But Indian life was attractive
for other values—for social equality, mobility, adventure, and, as two
adult converts acknowledged, "the most perfect freedom, the ease
of living, [and] the absence of those cares and corroding solicitudes
which so often prevail with us." . . .as Crevecoeur said, there must
have been in the Indians' "social bond something singularly captivat-
ing." Whatever it was, its power had no better measure than the large
number of English colonists who became, contrary to the civilized
assumptions of their countrymen, white Indians.[101]

This statement Rand made to the cadet reveals a powerful, if hidden, continuity between the Rand libertarians adore and the Nietzschean advocate of the strong sacrificing the weaker to fulfill their
desires that she carried with her to America. In her first edition of *We
the Living*, her first American novel, she presents an argument between
Kira, her heroine, and a communist. Kira denounces the communist
sacrifice of the distinguished for the good of the "masses." Her own
view is different:

What are your masses but mud to be ground under foot, fuel to be
burned for those who deserve it? What is the people but millions of
puny, shriveled, helpless souls that have no thoughts of their own, no
dreams of their own, no will of their own, who eat and sleep and chew
helplessly the words others put into their mildewed brains . . . I know
of no worse injustice than justice for all.[102]

These disturbing passages were excised from the second edition, and
are almost unknown today, leading many to think she overcame her
Nietzschean contempt for most people. Her reasoning about Indians

demonstrates that this nihilistic contempt colored her thought throughout her life in America.

Rand erred on the side of the powerful dominating the less powerful. A true friend of rights would have erred in the other direction. Rand
justified theft and murder to create *Lebensraum* against people she knew
nothing about. (This word is fair as the Nazis cited America's example of
killing Indians in justifying their own policies)

For a woman who claimed all moral issues were "a code of black and white"
and "objective," how can this be?[103] What could be more relativistic than rec-
ognizing rights only when people acted in a way she approved of, and had
proven it to her? Clearly, Rand was blinded by confusions that lurked at the
heart of her philosophy. Those confusions were her inability to recognize the
central importance of empathy and relationships in making the individuals
she admired possible and in sustaining them. Had she fully integrated this,
she would have recognized the weakness of building a moral philosophy on
abstractions far removed from human beings, abstractions to which she could
then sacrifice real human beings if she judged them not sufficiently "rational."

Small wonder that libertarianism in its many forms has had such a
mixed and often extraordinarily negative impact upon our country and
upon the individuals and freedom it claims to honor.

CONCLUSION

*We have reversed the libertarians' criticisms of many progressives being "col-
lectivists" who support aggression against peaceful people. We argue it is
they who do not understand what an individual is. It is they who do not
understand many truly terrible forms of coercion, and can only perceive it
when a gun is pointed at them. And, as Ayn Rand showed, not always even
then. Apparently, it is also they who do not understand what it is to be a
human being of moderate to low income and subordinate to another, anywhere in the United States, now or in the past. In the name of individualism
and freedom they would subordinate real individuals and concrete freedoms
to the collective power of capitalism. Libertarianism has become an apology*

for a form of collectivism that reflects only a portion of what it is to be a human being, and sacrifices the rest of who we are to it.

We agree with libertarians that the United States' corrupt collusions of government and wealth, of the military and defense industries, is bad and should end. But that does not mean the government's tasks should not be performed at all. Tasks such as civil rights protection, including protection against sexual harassment or bad employment conditions, are means for ending or reducing coercion in relationships brought about by systemically unequal power. There are many such examples with respect to both people and the environment. We need more than slogans and vague promises about the "magic of the market" when the entire past history of the market in real societies suggests our worries are very well founded.

When libertarians choose to broaden their understanding of what an individual really is and what property really is, they will be in a position to contribute importantly to this vital task. Until then, libertarianism in theory praises what is voluntary while in practice defends authoritarian relations in business, praises enormous inequalities between people seeking to enter into equal relationships, demonstrates blindness to ecological questions not easily reduced to property rights and money profit, and demonstrates still more blindness to abuses of the powerless by the powerful through their greater ability to twist society's rules and practices in their favor.

NOTES

49 Fisher, Marc. "Public or Private Space? Line Blurs in Silver Spring." *The Washington Post.* June 21, 2007. www.washingtonpost.com/wp-dyn/content/article/2007/06/20/AR2007062002354.html

50 Rand, Ayn. *For the New Intellectual.* New York: New American Library, 1961, p. 55.

51 Tucille, Jerome. *It Usually Begins With Ayn Rand, 25th Anniversary Edition.* New York: Fox and Wilkes, 1997.

52 These statistics come from two excellent biographies of Rand: Heller, Anne C. *Ayn Rand and the World She Made.* New York: Doubleday,

2009; Burns, Jennifer. *Goddess of the Market: Ayn Rand and the American Right*. Oxford: Oxford University Press, 2009.

54 Heller, op. cit., p. xii.

55 Rand, Ayn. *Atlas Shrugged*, New York: Penguin, 1992, p. 989.

56 *Atlas Shrugged*. New York: Plume, 1999, p. 1070.

57 *Atlas Shrugged*, op. cit. 1992, p. 944.

58 von Mises quoted in *Goddess of the Market: Ayn Rand and the American Right*, p. 177.

59 Rothbard's perceptive criticism is discussed in both biographies of Ayn Rand: Burns, op. cit., p. 153; Heller, op. cit. p. 253.

60 Heller, op. cit., p. 298.

61 Ibid., pp. 302–303

62 See the discussion in Burns, op. cit., pp. 40–41.

64 Rand, Ayn. *Fountainhead*. New York: Signet, 1993, p. 606.

65 Heller, op. cit., p. 303.

66 Friedman, Milton. "The Social Responsibility of Business is to Increase its Profits." *The New York Times Magazine*. Sept. 13, 1970. www.colorado. edu/studentgroups/libertarians/issues/friedman-soc-resp-business.html

67 On the Kochs and Indians, see: webarchives.net/december_1999/koch_ loses_oil_fraud_case.htm

68 Berger, Peter and Thomas Luckmann. *The Social Construction of Reality: A Treatise on the Sociology of Knowledge*. New York: Anchor, 1967.

69 Rand, Ayn. *The Virtue of Selfishness*. New York: Signet, 1964, p. 34.

70 Ibid., p. 61.

71 Lewis, Paul, Peter Berger, and his critics. "The Significance of Emergence." *Society*. 47: 3, 2010. pp. 207–213.

72 Yevtushenko, Yevgeny. "People." *Selected Poems*. New York: Penguin, 1979, p. 85.

73 Hume, David. "An Inquiry Concerning the Principles of Morals, appendix II." *Moral and Political Philosophy*. Henry D. Aiken, ed. New York: Hafner, 1948, p. 270.

74 Smith, Adam. *The Theory of Moral Sentiments*. New Rochelle, NY: Arlington House, 1969, p. 10; Hume, op. cit., "Of Self Love," pp. 270–275.

75 Hume, "Treatise on Human Nature, Bk. II, sec. ii," op. cit., p. 7.

76 Smith, op. cit., p. 125.

77 Hume, "Treatise on Human Understanding, Pt. II, sec. vi; Sec. ix," op. cit., pp. 227, 258. See also Henry Aiken's introductory essay, pp. xxiii.

I am uncertain whether Aiken clarified what is implicit in Hume, as it certainly is, or whether Hume fully grasped this point himself, for in Pt. II, Sec. v he noted "It is needless to push our researches so far as to ask why we have humanity or a fellow feeling with others" (p. 212).

78   Hume, "Treatise on Human Nature, Bk. III, Part. II, sec. I," op. cit., p. 52.

79   Fisher, John A. "Taking Sympathy Seriously: A Defense of Our Moral Psychology Toward Animals." *The Animal Rights/Environmental Ethics Debate.* ed. Eugene Hargrove. Albany: State University of New York Press, 1992, pp. 227–248; Callicott, J. Baird. "Animal Liberation and Environmental Ethics: Back Together Again." *In Defense of the Land Ethic: Essays in Environmental Philosophy.* Albany: State University of New York Press, 1989, pp. 49–59.

80   Leopold, Ido. *Sand County Almanac.* New York: Ballantine Books, 1970, p. 117.

81   Quoted by Worster, Donald. *The Economy of Nature: A History of Ecological Ideas.* Cambridge: Cambridge University Press, 1977, p. 181.

82   Darwin, Charles. *The Descent of Man.* New York: Modern Library, pp. 471–511, esp. 492. See also: Callicott, op. cit., p. 119; Worster, *Nature's Economy,* op. cit., pp. 180–184; Nash, Roderick. *The Rights of Nature: A History of Environmental Ethics.* Madison: University of Wisconsin Press, 1989, pp. 42–45.

83   Hayek, F. A. *Law, Legislation and Liberty, Vol. 2: The Mirage of Social Justice.* Chicago: University of Chicago Press, 1976, p. 117.

84   Locke, John. *Two Treatises on Government.* Peter Laslett, ed. New York: Mentor, 1960, p. 327–344.

85   Rothbard, Murray N. *Law, Property Rights and Air Pollution.* Ludwig von Mises Institute, 2006. mises.org/daily/2120

86   Hall, Janet, Victor Brajer, and Frederick W. Lurmann. *The Benefits of Meeting Federal Clean Air Standards in the South Coast and San Joaquin Valley Air Basins.* Fullerton: California State University, 2008, p. 84.

87   Watson, Steve. "Libertarian Talk Radio Activist Jailed for 100 Days for Having a Couch in His Yard." *Alex Jones Infowars.* Nov. 17, 2008. infowars.net/articles/november2008/171108Freeman.htm

88   See in particular: diZerega, Gus. "Spontaneous Order and Liberalism's Complex Relation to Democracy." *The Independent Review.* 16:2, Fall, 2011.

89   Publius (Madison, James). "Federalist 58." *The Federalist Papers.* Clinton Rossiter, ed. New York: Penguin, 1961, p. 361.

90   "Meteor Blades, Got AIDs? Your fault, says Ron Paul. Boss can't keep his hands off you? Switch jobs, says Ron Paul." *Daily Kos.* Dec. 10, 2011. www.dailykos.com/story/2011/12/30/1049973/-Got-AIDs-Your-fault,-says-Ron-Paul-Boss-cant-keep-his-hands-off-you-Switch-jobs,-says-Ron-Paul?via=blog_1

91   Sanchez, Julian. "Cato and the Kochs: A Presignation Letter." *Julian Sanchez.* March 5, 2012. www.juliansanchez.com/2012/03/05/cato-and-the-kochs-a-presignation-letter/

92   "Koch Loses Oil Fraud Case." December 1999. www.channelingreality.com/Temp_Dir/Reason_Koch/Koch%20Oil.pdf

93   Nozick, Robert. *Anarchy, State, and Utopia,* Hoboken: Wiley-Blackwell, 2001, p. 290–292.

94   www.huffingtonpost.com/2009/09/28/mom-goes-blind-so-her-dau_n_301947.html

95   Murray Rothbard grasped this point quite clearly. See his *Ethics of Liberty,* ch. 19, "Property Rights and the Theory of Contracts." mises.org/rothbard/ethics/nineteen.asp

96   en.wikipedia.org/wiki/Triangle_Shirtwaist_Factory_fire; www.ilr.cornell.edu/trianglefire/

97   Davidson, Carl. *New Paths to Socialism: Essays on the Mondragón Cooperatives and Workplace Democracy, Green Manufacturing, Structural Reform, and the Politics of Transition.* Pittsburg: Changemaker Publications, 2011.

98   Rand, Ayn. *The Virtue of Selfishness.* New York: Signet, 1964, p. 30.

99   Rand, Ayn. *Ayn Rand Answers: The Best of Her Q & A.* New York: NAL Trade, 2005, p. 103–104.

100 Ironically, a libertarian think tank offers a telling rebuttal to Rand. See: Rodriguez, Carlos, Craig Galbraith, and Curt Stiles. "American Indian Collectivism: Past Myth Present Reality." *Property and Environment Research Center.* Bozeman, MT, 2006. www.perc.org/articles/article802.php

101 Axtell, James. "The White Indians of Colonial America." *The William and Mary Quarterly, Third Series.* 32:1, Jan. 1975, p. 88.

102 Rand, Ayn. *We the Living,* quoted in: Sciabarra, Chris Matthew. *Ayn Rand the Russian Radical.* University Park, PA: University of Pennsylvania Press, 1995, p. 101.

103 Rand, Ayn. "The Cult of Moral Grayness." *The Virtue of Selfishness,* op. cit., p. 92.

CHAPTER FIVE

HOW LIBERTARIANISM SEDUCES AMERICANS AWAY FROM DEMOCRACY

By Julianne E. Maurseth

OVERVIEW: WHY THE SEDUCTION IS APPEALING

This chapter offers a depth psychology perspective regarding how and why libertarianism is wooing more and more Americans away from a commitment to democracy. The following assumptions are made:

1. Libertarian philosophy splits in half the American commitment to "liberty and justice for all." It keeps "liberty" and throws "justice" away as irrelevant.

2. American historical memory is fraught with unacknowledged grief for violence and social injustice based on centuries of racial and class oppression.

3. Continued lack of acknowledgement and responsibility for social injustice is evidenced today, for example, by increasing rates of incarceration of Americans of color, increasing rates of American children living in poverty, and increasing U.S. bombardments of civilians in other countries.

4. A gross level of social injustice weighs on the collective American psyche, primarily at an unconscious level.

5. The unconscious, troubled human psyche seeks ways to rid itself of what troubles it.

6. Libertarian philosophy offers a way out of the "trouble" of feeling basic human concern for those suffering from social injustice by rationalizing all evidence of such injustice as *individual* problems of inadequacy, for which the solution is always and only greater individual "liberty."

7. Psychological maturation requires we face our collective troubles squarely and develop systemic solutions together as a society.

8. Libertarian philosophy retards Americans' psychological maturation by providing excuses to avoid social responsibility for fellow citizens' suffering.

9. The requirements of the human psyche are archetypal, thus more ancient than libertarian philosophy. We had better heed the psyche's requirements to mature as a society, or we risk losing our democracy for a smug and pathetic substitute.

SEEING THE COMMONS WITHIN OUR PSYCHE

"It would all be so much simpler if we could only deny the existence of the psyche," Carl Jung[104] counsels us.

In the original Greek, *psyche* was the term for both soul and butterfly, implying the liquefaction of the caterpillar in its cocoon as the equivalent of the voracious human before it is initiated into an entirely different life: the human soul. The storyteller Michael Meade[105] has another way of saying it, "The road of certain death and greater life appear together," where initiation, that archetypal requirement for a mature human psyche, insists we bend low, break down, die, and find out what we are that connects us inseparably to a larger life that we did not even know was possible. Ignorance of this larger life does not make it disappear.

We are living in an era of dangerous ignorance about this larger life, including ignorance of our interdependence with all people and the natural world. America has a peculiar claim to such ignorance because uninitiated American identity is developmentally stuck in adolescence and wrapped around being individualistic to the point of peril to itself and others—like a teenager driving 120mph on a crowded freeway. Initiation is an ancient rite in which adolescents experience a death, or liquefaction, of their former identity in order to open up to an enlarged identity and responsibility to community. We Americans urgently need new initiations for our times so that we grow up as a national culture. Our hearts and souls need to open to recognize our connections to each other, to the natural world, and to the deeper meaning of America beyond making money.

This is not a chapter about theology, but about democracy—and about whether we Americans have the maturity of soul to fight for it and persist through the challenges of escalating attacks on our democracy. It is important to clarify what democracy *is,* since the attacks on it are at least in part based on dueling definitions of democracy.

As an American, I believe a larger life calls to us through the very name democracy. I do not think the American Dream was ever about the stereotype of owning a home, sending the kids to college, and retiring well off, but about the potential for a human community to mature in such a way that "liberty and justice for all" could become a reality. Material comforts may have been the cultural evidence of some degree of "liberty and justice," but the archetype of democracy within the human psyche is too large to be confined by economic definitions or accumulation.

Consequently, I am using the term "democracy" as a powerful paradox requiring maturity of soul in order to responsibly and consciously hold the inherent tensions[106] that exist between individual liberty and social justice. America has not yet mastered and may never master the maturity of soul required to hold this tension responsibly as a nation under all circumstances, if such mastery is even possible. At certain times America has led the world in a vision of what democracy can be and should aim to become. America has been an inspiration for other nations specifically because of our commitment to the ideal of "liberty and justice for all." Not just one or the other—but both simultaneously.

It is now questionable whether we still inspire, despite much rhetoric that we do. My proposal is that America's inspiration is weakening in direct proportion to our weakening commitment to "liberty and justice for all," and that increasing numbers of Americans are losing heart for this paradoxical ideal. This loss of heart by individual Americans comes from many factors, some of which are being deliberately promoted by political and economic interests that would benefit from more Americans giving up the fight for democracy.

Democracy, from the Greek root *demokratia,* means "rule of the people." Over millennia of time—from Cleisthenes, the "father of democracy" in 6th century B.C. Athens, where citizen assemblies were established, to the Cossack republics in the Middle Ages that elected their representatives, to England's Magna Carta restricting a king's rule and protecting citizens' freedom from unlawful imprisonment, to the French Revolution overthrowing the royal court of Versailles, to the American Revolution overthrowing the rule of King George, to the creation of the United States' Constitution and its "balance of powers" in government, to the testing of America's commitment to democracy in the Civil War of the 1860s and again in the civil rights movement of the 1960s, to the global outcry against state violence in China's Tiananmen Square, to the persistent peaceful assembly of Egyptian citizens in Tahrir Square until Mubarak was overthrown, to the Occupy Wall Street movement spreading to eighty countries in less than two months—the "rule of the people" has been undergoing an evolution in human consciousness and action.

Democracy is not and has never been perfect anywhere. Is that any reason to give up on it? What if we're learning as evolving human beings—as if we're in a democracy experiment?

Our human engagement with democracy is quite astounding and beautiful. The erratic evolution of democracy is evidence of a particular kind of beauty alive in the human soul, the psyche, which endures across time, place, obstacle, and circumstance. It indicates that we humans have a capacity to return to—and possibly persist in—democracy.

If this is possible, then "democracy" is not a fixed system, but an archetype working like yeast across millennia in the collective human psyche,[107] leavening our awareness of our mutual actions and mutual impacts on the Commons of society and the natural world. As an archetype, democracy would exude a persistent pressure on the collective human psyche to "consciously evolve," as Barbara Marx Hubbard[108] uses the term. It may also exude a persistent pressure to collectively learn how to ethically wield the immense power we humans have over each other and our natural environment within our shared Commons.

What if learning how to implement the paradoxical ideal of democracy is the archetypal story of America? What if now is the nation's developmental time to give up the old caterpillar definitions of national identity in order to break down, bend low, and die to what we thought we were so that the larger life of "liberty and justice for all" can be formed and emerge through us? Will we allow this difficult development, or will the ideal die in the cocoon?

America has faced intense pressure to learn democracy and evolve "in liberty and justice for all" many times before—when we abolished slavery, when we gave women the right to vote, when we passed the Civil Rights Act and then the Voting Rights Act. We face another critical juncture and dramatic choice now that aims straight at the heart of who we are as Americans:

Are we capable of defending our democracy as "liberty and justice for all"?
Or are we going to let democracy be dismantled for money?

The voracious caterpillars are up at night, munching, munching, munching away on our democracy's Bill of Rights, laws, and institutions, doing all they can to privatize our publicly-held Commons in order to generate new investments in the stock market and fuel ever-higher corporate profits. They justify their actions through the use of ideologies that are anti-democratic at the core, and which, wittingly or unwittingly, more and more Americans appear to support.

WHY WOULD AMERICANS BE SWAYED BY AN ANTI-DEMOCRATIC IDEOLOGY?

In examining this question, we will look at the curious influence of libertarian ideology, its one-sided view of democracy, and its association with Ayn Rand's Objectivist philosophy. These ideas actually invite Americans to stay frozen at the caterpillar stage of development, thereby resisting a larger life of interdependence with others. Ignorance of this larger life does not make it disappear. Our ignorance merely drives our interdependence more deeply into our nation's Shadow,[109] where our stubborn resistance to it causes us to bicker like Tweedledee and Tweedledum, doing battle over a rattle.

The longer we refuse to bend low, break down, die, and find out what we are as a nation that connects us inseparably to a larger life, the longer we refuse to mature our nation's soul, the faster will be the undoing of our democracy. Will we let that happen?

IS DEMOCRACY *REALLY* BEING DISMANTLED?

Lest you think my framing of the matter too dramatic, here are a few examples of escalating attacks on American democracy and our Commons:

> ➤ *The bi-partisan passage of the Patriot Act in 2001 under the Bush administration, and subsequent renewals under the Obama administration, which suspended the writ of habeas corpus that protects citizens from unlawful arrest or being held without a trial, allowed increasing invasions of privacy and weakened our Bill of Rights. Increasingly, Americans are being accused of "terrorism" for practicing their First Amendment rights.*

➤ *The sell-off of public ownership of airwaves in radio and television stations to private corporations such as Clear Channel, and the public media deregulation under the Clinton administration, without public approval.*

➤ *The Supreme Court's 2010 "Citizens United" ruling that money is free speech, which gave carte blanche to Political Action Committees (PACs) to not only buy elections, but also withhold the names of contributors to the PACs. The result: over one billion dollars poured in from PACs to influence the 2012 elections without the transparency needed for the public to know who was behind the messaging in advertisements.*

➤ *In March 2011, Michigan governor Rick Snyder signed into law Public Act 4, the "Emergency Manager" law that allows the governor to appoint non-elected officials in cities facing financial hardship. The Emergency Manager is not beholden to the public, but is allowed to make all municipal decisions, eliminate the elected city council, sell off public assets such as city parks and public schools to private owners, break union contracts, take over pension systems, set school curricula, and dissolve entire municipalities.[110] The cities of Benton Harbor, Flint, Inkster, and Pontiac have already been taken over by Emergency Managers.*

➤ *In 2011 alone, 180 bills were introduced in forty-one states to restrict voter registration and to eliminate early voting and absentee voting. Thousands of citizens were purged from voting records, and the patterns indicated that the purged names were disproportionately Latinos, African-Americans, elderly, youth, and Democrats. Investigations in Florida revealed, among other examples, that a 91-year-old WWII veteran was purged from voter registration rolls.*

➤ *Privatization of our public schools from elementary to university levels, and the demonization of teachers, is accelerating across nearly every state. Public assets of land, libraries, art collections, and more are being sold off from public university campuses,*

> *while increasing numbers of young children are in "virtual*
> *schools" on their home computers, without any face-to-face*
> *teacher interaction.*
> ➤ *Usurious debt of college student loans at one trillion dollars is*
> *weighing down our nation's youth, while the far Right seeks to*
> *raise the interest rates on student loans even higher.*

We've got a problem, folks. Something core to America has gone awry in our nation. Deeper than an economic debate yet intertwined with economic ideology is an ethical and moral imperative to make our nation live up to its commitment to "liberty and justice for all." We've evolved toward democracy before and we can do it again. Yet these examples above indicate we're heading far away from that commitment—and at breakneck speed.

The main reason why libertarianism needs examining is because it divides this commitment to democracy in half—keeping only "liberty for all" and discarding "justice for all" as foolish. To the libertarian, because the implementation of "justice for all" has been unsuccessful so far, that proves it cannot work. Their conclusions are tautological. With such limited vision and flawed logic, our nation would never have been born. In fact, libertarianism represents the inability to hold the paradoxical tension of this high ideal and work toward it to improve its democratic systems of delivery.

Instead, libertarians are committed to dismantling the systems of delivery held in common, as in the examples listed above.

When you think libertarian, don't just think of Ron Paul with his consistent, principled message across decades. Also think of the Koch brothers on the board of the Cato Institute, a Libertarian think tank. In 1980, David Koch ran on the libertarian ticket as candidate for vice president, with Edward Clark as presidential candidate. Also think of Paul Ryan, an Ayn Rand follower, who became chairman of the House Budget Committee in 2011 and a vice presidential candidate on the Republican ticket in 2012. His Ryan Plan included drastic cuts to the national Commons and the dismantling of democratic systems of delivery that would have made Rand proud. Also think of many Ayn Rand Objectivist acolytes who find libertarianism to be more aligned with their values than the major political parties, despite the fact that Rand herself detested libertarians.[111]

Libertarians with money and power, such as the Koch brothers, have been reweaving the fabric of American policy, law, budgets, public education, and other social services for decades. The only government regulation libertarians do support is exactly the same as that which Ayn Rand favored: the police, the military, and the courts. Otherwise, they seek to eliminate nearly all else provided by government services.

Although the libertarian tent covers a broad assortment of views, these views tend to coalesce around a core ideology that is not synched up with democratic principles.

THE SELF-JUSTIFYING LOOP OF LIBERTARIAN IDEOLOGY

The Libertarian Party was officially started in 1971 by David Nolan and a few of his friends. They were angered by the Vietnam War, as well as by Nixon's wage and price controls and his removal of the gold standard. *The New York Times*[112] reported in 2010, at the time of Nolan's death at 66 years of age:

> *David Fraser Nolan was born on Nov. 23, 1943, in Washington and grew up in Maryland. He was influenced by the individualist fiction of Robert A. Heinlein and the novels of Ayn Rand. He went to Massachusetts Institute of Technology with the idea of being an uncompromising architect like Howard Roark, the hero of Rand's "Fountainhead."*
>
> *. . . When the Libertarian Party was formed, Mr. Nolan emphasized the need for liberals and conservatives to unite behind unrestricted capitalism and maximum civil liberties.*

"Unrestricted capitalism and maximum civil liberties" remain the Libertarian Party's core ideology today. The preamble[113] to the Party platform states:

As libertarians, we seek a world of liberty; a world in which all individuals are sovereign over their own lives and no one is forced to sacrifice his or her values for the benefit of others.

We believe that respect for individual rights is the essential precondition for a free and prosperous world, that force and fraud must be banished from human relationships, and that only through freedom can peace and prosperity be realized.

Consequently, we defend each person's right to engage in any activity that is peaceful and honest, and welcome the diversity that freedom brings. The world we seek to build is one where individuals are free to follow their own dreams in their own ways, without interference from government or any authoritarian power.

In the following pages we have set forth our basic principles and enumerated various policy stands derived from those principles. These specific policies are not our goal, however. Our goal is nothing neither more nor less than a world set free in our lifetime, and it is to this end that we take these stands.

Well, now: who but an authoritarian would argue with these views? They sound so reasonable to the progressive ear. The Party's stand on personal liberty is why they support homosexual rights, abortion choice, and de-criminalization of drug use. They are ideologically consistent and thorough in articulating how the principle of personal liberty should translate into social policy, as long as people "do not forcibly interfere with the equal rights of others to live in whatever manner they choose."

Their ideological consistency of "live and let live" is progressive. But the second major facet of libertarian ideology—commitment to laissez-faire economics—leads in the opposite direction of their goal for "a world set free in our lifetime."

There is a reason why libertarianism cuts the democracy ideal in half and throws away "justice for all." Social justice does not jive with unregulated capitalism. In fact, unregulated capitalism leads in a straight line to social injustice and environmental degradation. You can bet on it. This is not simply a Marxist argument, although Marx and others made similar points. It is also an argument based on the facts of how unregulated capitalism actually works.

The fact is, it is *long past time to stop reactively labeling anything which critiques unregulated capitalism as "unjust"—as socialism, communism, or a welfare state.* We need to begin opening our minds to economic possibilities beyond the false dichotomy of *either* unregulated capitalism *or* state-regulated socialism. The continuous propagation of this false dichotomy shuts down all consideration of potential alternatives. A closed mind needs self-justification to stay closed.

Libertarian ideology performs several self-justifications to avoid looking at the unjust social impacts of laissez-faire economics and remain within a self-sealing loop. Three of these oft-repeated self-justifications are listed below:

1. Business has never been "truly" 100% unregulated, and therefore the problems we've had with irresponsible businesses are the result of too much regulation instead of the self-correcting mechanisms of the free market.

2. Environmental degradation will eventually be corrected by "free markets and property rights" which "stimulate the technological innovations and behavioral changes required to protect our environment and ecosystems." Therefore, the more we privatize public lands the more we protect the environment because "Governments, unlike private businesses, are unaccountable for such damage done to our environment and have a terrible track record when it comes to environmental protection."

3. Human nature is fixed in self-interest and relatively unchanging. Only free market opportunities release latent individual abilities, which are there from the beginning. As a starting point, people should be equal under the law. Yet because they are not equal in abilities, they will not be equal in personal outcomes as an ending point. The welfare state, such as was

created under FDR's New Deal, assumes that people are "plastic," are shaped by their environments and can improve when provided with adequate resources and social services. This is foolish because it is incorrect. It wastes the resources of the people who earned them by giving to others who did not earn them and will not use the resources well.

To grasp why these three points are self-sealing, it is important to understand the different historical eras and contexts libertarianism draws upon to construct its ideology. On the one hand, its commitment to individual liberty has theoretical roots in "liberalism," a major philosophy of the eighteenth-century Enlightenment era that valued the rights and autonomy of the individual. On the other hand, its commitment to laissez-faire capitalism has theoretical roots in prior eras, dating back to thirteenth-century Europe when "business for business's sake was born,"[114] and the rising merchant class found ways around trade regulations and controls, as well as ways to market the goods produced by craftsmen so that the merchants' profits were increased and labor costs were kept as low as possible.

In human history, capitalism preceded the widespread cause of individual liberty. Into an existing economic system that already worked well for the elite class grew a passion among intellectuals for the rights of individual, propertied men who were not of "royal" blood. This has been a process, mind you, of enlarging the human circle for exactly who is considered human and what percentage of that human is considered an autonomous individual.

Later rhapsodies of why "the free market must be free" as an expression of individual freedom were added onto the predatory practices of capitalism to justify and attempt to hide its brutality. The work of neuroscientist Joseph LeDoux indicates ". . . we do things and then make up stories to explain what we've done so that it seems consistent with our view of who we are and what our lives are like."[115] The man of freedom, proclaiming the rights of all men to be free, would have a hard time justifying a brutal economic system that included slavery. Then in 1776 came Adam Smith's *Wealth of Nations* and in 1859 came Charles Darwin's *The Origin of Species*. Both of these works were distorted and twisted to fit the economic argument that the free market must be free and were used to justify the ethics of the capitalist—no matter the result.

It was proclaimed that Smith said human nature was based on self-interest. He did not say that. It was proclaimed that Darwin said the species who survive are the most aggressive, most competitive, or "fit," hence the term "survival of the fittest." He did not say that. Nevertheless, these ideas are now Biblical dogma to free market believers, including libertarians.

Let's be clear: capitalism is not "evil." That is not the point, nor is it even vaguely a useful or valid argument. But advocating for unregulated capitalism is absurd because it assumes that those very advocates are somehow themselves not partisan, and that people are not influencing the conditions of the market itself. That is a silly, naïve assumption. It ignores the uses of people's power to persuade, distort, convert, and control the conditions of a "market" for their own ends, and ignores how many generations of people may suffer until the perpetrators are somehow revealed and stopped. Look how fast 180 bills were introduced in forty-one states in 2011 alone to restrict the basic American right of voter registration. What does the ideology of the "free market" offer to the citizen whose name was purged from a list of voters? Only the mechanisms of social justice have a solution.

Libertarians see government taxes collected from people with productive outcomes and given to benefit people with less productive outcomes as in essence taking "the fruits of their labor." The Libertarian Party platform states, "All efforts by government to redistribute wealth, or to control or manage trade, are improper in a free society."

Improper? This is a fascinating use of the word. If the term "improper" means the violation of moral and ethical standards, then let's consider two examples of free market impropriety and how libertarian self-justification, such as the three points explained above, keeps impropriety and injustice going strong.

Example #1: Our increasingly privatized, free-market prison system now incarcerates more African-American men than were slaves before the Civil War.[116] On the one hand, since a high percentage of prisoners are incarcerated for drug possession, and libertarians are in favor of decriminalizing drug possession, their platform would solve this problem, if adopted, by reducing the number of people arrested for drug possession in the first place. Yet libertarians' contradictory support of the free market would inherently include support for the privatization of prisons and the ability of the prison corporations to self-regulate—meaning that the prison corporation makes profits by: (a) increasing the number of inmates; (b) decreasing the number of guards; (c) keeping guard pay and benefits as low as possible; (d) hiring out inmates' labor to other private corporations at literal slave wage prices; and (e) minimizing costs and variety of inmates' resources and supplies—all to compete in a "free, unregulated market."

Example #2: During the 2010 disaster in the Gulf of Mexico, British Petroleum was concerned about harming its reputation, its profits, and consequently its stock price in the "free market." So, often under cover of night, and in violation of being ordered to stop, it sprayed an even more toxic chemical across the oil slick on the ocean to sink all evidence and limit its liabilities for clean-up costs. Today, Gulf fisherman bring out of the ocean shrimp with no eyes, crabs with no claws, and fish with uncovered gills. Twelve men are dead from the Deepwater Horizon rig explosion, and the numbers keep rising for how many people in the Gulf are sick from toxic environmental poisoning. BP is back in the saddle with television ads proclaiming its commitment to the environment and new project proposals for yet more deep-water drilling.

Libertarian ideology needs an upgrade. It has no viable solutions for dealing with these two examples because each requires social justice action, which they abhor. Libertarianism is stuck back in its 1970s roots, when corporations were not yet running the government to the extent they are now, with four to five industry lobbyists for every elected representative in Congress. A question that needs an answer: *Why does the opening libertarian principle on the Party's website "challenge the cult of the omnipotent state," but not challenge the cult of the omnipotent corporation?*

In addition, libertarianism is stuck even further back in eighteenth century Enlightenment views of "liberalism," which justifiably attacked the State as oppressing the basic human rights of the individual. Yes, that was true when the State was the *only* problem but, in case libertarians haven't noticed, the State has been taken over by the rule of corporations.

Libertarians, listen up: you cannot have your ideological cake and eat it, too. You cannot stand upon your insistence that social justice hasn't worked, therefore it needs to be abandoned, and at the same time claim that the principle of unregulated capitalism is to be followed without reservation because, even though it hasn't yet worked, *it would work if we'd just let it.*

Why wouldn't that also be the logical case with the principle of social justice?

Is it because you, my libertarian friend, do not want to pay for the costs of social justice and its questionable results?

What if I do not want to pay for the costs of the "free market" and its questionable results?

How shall we work this out as citizens together in a democracy?

HOW THE "FREE MARKET" IMPACTS AMERICANS' PERSISTENCE IN DEMOCRACY

Messy, frustrating, time-consuming: democracy requires that citizens persist with each other, not only because democratic principles are worth the struggle, but because the outcomes have the potential to elevate society and all of its citizens in the process. Whether or not this potential is realized depends, perhaps entirely, on the persistence of its citizens to be accountable—and to hold their elected representatives accountable—to democratic principles. Persistence requires a willingness to muck about together, debate and learn new ideas together, and assert democracy's core paradox for both individual freedom and social justice simultaneously.

I'm concerned that, despite the commitment of some Americans to democracy's ideal, including the commitment of the Occupy movement, the willingness of many other Americans to persist is weakening. Various data points indicate something is afoot. More voters have elected representatives to office who oppose social justice. Membership in the Libertarian Party is increasing. And American readership of Ayn Rand's works rose dramatically after the 2008 financial crises, with sales of *Atlas Shrugged* tripling in 2009 over the prior year at 600,000 copies.[117] Why?

What underlying factors might possibly be causing Americans to give up on the democracy ideal itself, and seek out alternatives that divorce social justice from individual liberty?

Among many possible factors, I propose here only three. Each reflects systemic impacts on Americans' daily lives that have worn many people down, making them less available to democracy and less willing to protect it. Libertarians' insistence on individual liberty might analyze these factors as solely the individual's responsibility for being worn down, but democracy's ideal that includes social justice also requires that we examine the systemic impacts across society.

Factor #1: Americans are physically exhausted from overwork and less sleep

Democracy depends on active, continuous citizen participation. How can Americans fulfill this need when they work more hours on average than people of any other nation?

Not surprisingly, over the last 20 years, a large number of U.S. employees report being overworked. A 2004 study found that 44 percent of respondents were often or very often overworked, overwhelmed at their job, or unable to step back and process what's going on. A third reported being chronically overworked. These overworked employees had much higher stress levels, worse physical health, higher rates of

*depression, and reduced ability to take care of themselves and their
less-pressured colleagues. Adverse effects of long hours, stress, and
overwork have been found in a number of studies, for a variety of
physical, mental, and social health outcomes.*[118]

Because of overwork, Americans are increasingly sleep-deprived. Data
from the National Sleep Foundation[119] indicates:

*Spending an average of 4.5 hours each week doing additional work
from home on top of a 9.5 average workday, Americans are working
more and trying to cope with the resulting daytime sleepiness. In fact
63% state they are likely to just accept their sleepiness and keep going.*

*Of those taking their work home with them, 20% say they spend
10 or more additional hours each week and 25% spend at least 7
additional hours each week on job-related duties. Almost one-quar-
ter (23%) of all respondents did job-related work in the hour before
going to bed at least a few nights each week.*

*Working too much and sleeping too little takes a serious toll on
people's professional and personal lives.*

How can people persist in democracy as engaged citizens when they
are increasingly physically exhausted by work and have less time for their
own lives? The patience and open-mindedness necessary in a participative democracy is in short supply when citizens are worn down by sleep-
deprivation from overwork.

In 1991, economist Juliet Schor revealed in *The Overworked American*[120] that across the prior two decades, Americans' work time increased
by one full month per year, pressured by industrial claims that American productivity would lag behind the global economy unless Americans
worked more. In the last two decades, Americans' working hours have
continued rising.

How has all this hard work benefitted Americans from the standpoint
of social justice? As we know too well, most of the financial gains since

1980 have increasingly gone into the pockets of corporate executives and swollen the stock portfolios of the wealthy, while Americans' income on average has stayed flat when adjusted for inflation. Under the Reagan administration, 1980 was the start of the deliberate dismantling of our democracy's ideals, laws, and infrastructure, including the deregulation of capitalism. In 1980, libertarians were already hard at work, separating systems of social justice from liberty.

Factor #2: It is very difficult to see systemic causes when you're in them, and it's typical to blame only a part of the complex problem

You may know the example of the "boiled frog," but it goes like this: if you place a frog in boiling water, it will jump out. But if you place a frog in cold water, and slowly turn up the heat, it will sit in the water and boil to death.

Overwork for the average America has been on a slow boil. Economic deregulations from industry lobbyists have been on a slow boil. The transformation of our nation from a democracy to a plutocracy has been on a slow boil. The indifference, impatience, or anger of many white Americans toward social justice causes for Americans of color and immigration rights has been on a slow boil. The incarceration rate—now the highest in the world, ahead of China and Russia, with over two million Americans in prison and nearly 6.7 million (1 of every 32) Americans held in the justice system in some manner[121]—has been on a slow boil.

These factors taken together indicate the total unraveling of our democracy. My contention is that the unraveling has been accelerating in proportion to Americans' tendency to place blame on only one part of a much larger systemic picture. For example, it is easier to blame a marginalized group of people who are different from you, such as immigrants, than it is to recognize how your own workplace and industry may be contributing directly to the dismantling of your rights by the financial investments and industry lobbying groups it supports.

Most Americans live a daily systemic contradiction between a non-democratic workplace and a so-called democratic society. Since most workplaces are not democracies, unless you are in a worker-owned cooperative, most Americans spend the majority of their waking hours fitting themselves into a workplace situation over which they have very little to no substantive control, except for the way they perform their own job. If they are fearful of losing their job, they may fit themselves into a situation that is unhealthy for them in many ways. Most people tend to accept this daily contradiction as a given, like an act of nature. But it is not a given. It could be different if people recognized that option, but *that requires a systemic perspective.*

Research indicates that most people have a tendency to blame themselves for the disadvantage they experience rather than to recognize any systemic causation as integral to their problems. Michael Lerner and his research team interviewed thousands of Americans across the political spectrum and confirmed this tendency.

We also discovered many people we interviewed blamed themselves for their sense of frustration or alienation. Many understood that their lack of fulfillment in their jobs was connected to the way that their workplace was structured, the powerlessness (in some jobs) or competitiveness (in other jobs) and the kind of "looking out for number one" that they foster. Yet they blamed themselves for having that kind of job in the first place. They imagined that if only they has worked harder when they were younger or been smarter or more attractive or more personable, they would have been out of this kind of job and into a far more satisfying one. Instead of understanding that very few jobs with meaning exist in this society, they believed that it was only people who had messed up their lives who would be faced with a work life that seemed so at variance with their own beliefs.[122]

Self-blame for the totality of one's own challenges in American work life synchs up with libertarian ideology that cuts social justice out of the picture. For any mature adult, personal responsibility is the necessary starting point. But, libertarianism would have it be the alpha and omega for solving all social ills. The more we see a systemic problem only in personal terms of effort or talent, the more likely we are to blame other individuals whom we identify as lacking the required effort or talent. In psychology, this is called "projection."

In the wake of the predatory sub-prime mortgage crisis, the airwaves were quickly filled with blame for the individuals who had signed their names to the loan agreements, rather than a systemic questioning of how and why the system had developed the predatory lending practices in the first place, deliberately and disproportionately targeting people of color. The tragedy to evicted families and to our systems of democracy is reflected in the following quote:

> More than ever, economic power seems today to have become political power, while citizens appear to be almost entirely stripped of their democratic defenses and their capacity to impress upon the political economy interests and demands that are incommensurable with those of capital owners.[123]

Unfortunately, there is a new trend of blame emerging—to pathologize an individual's righteous anger at systemic causes—further shutting down one's ability to recognize how the dismantling of democracy might be impacting one's own quality of life in America. The emotional, mental, and spiritual vacuum created when systemic context is absent stunts our awareness of a larger, shared society that is impacting all Americans.

Thus, our angry, blaming politics and national bickering accelerates.

Factor #3: Americans are emotionally exhausted from the bickering, incoherent media

Democracy depends on all citizens having regular access to coherent media that deliver factual information across a broad spectrum of ideas within context. Context increases the likelihood that citizens will understand the various issues and needs, even if they don't agree with them. Context is what enables us to see there is another point of view besides our own.

Today's media deliver most information with little to no context, and pander to the demographic audience they assume is watching. Citizens are bombarded with information without substance and, consequently, have less emotional and mental bandwidth available for persistent civic participation.

As corporate media continued consolidating under the Clinton administration, and as the ethical "firewall" between advertisers and the journalism newsroom was eliminated, so-called news has deteriorated to bickering instead of intelligent debate based on facts, research, and multiple viewpoints. This bickering is emotionally draining to citizen listeners who often tune it out by turning it off, or by selecting only a single source of information.

How can people persist in democracy when they are increasingly emotionally exhausted from bombardment by confounded media?

In addition, confusion among ideas poorly explained leaves Americans with hundreds of half-truths. One must become a research expert and scholar in order to tease out fact from fiction. No wonder Fox News is so popular—it digests and condenses information and makes it accessible in a world of confusion. Consider Glenn Beck's proclamation: "There is no such thing as society—there are only individuals." Beck provided no context for this statement—"There is no such thing as society"—which was a famous statement made by Margaret Thatcher, nor did he explain these views within a context of his agreement with Ayn Rand's philosophy. He simply stated it as "fact." Yet the strength of his assertion and its condensed digestibility fit within the limited bandwidth of an overwhelmed and physically exhausted person.

Lack of context and history serve to whittle the ideas down to nibs and bits, without relationship to a bigger picture. The resulting splinters generate more argument between supposed sides that are in reality mirror images of each other. While nearly all news across the political spectrum is offered to accommodate a narrow focus in limited time, our democracy is undermined.

When media does provide context, extended time is required to adequately present facts and ideas. Examples such as Bill Moyers' interviews, *60 Minutes*, and even the satirical investigations of Jon Stewart focus on developing past contexts and present impacts so that we can picture the potential future implications. The implications may be tragic, comic, or both, but with sufficient context presented to us we citizens can ponder and reflect instead of merely react.

On the Left in particular, another phenomenon arises that impacts the Left's capacity and willingness to defend democracy. Among some on the Left who see all forms of conflict as negative, there is an even greater aversion to the bickering, causing a retreat from civic participation entirely. One consequence of this viewpoint is the creation of a civic vacuum where such members withdraw their active political participation in order to protect themselves from involvement in conflicts.

Van Jones recently pointed out the difference in reaction, "You punch one of these right-wingers, they get mad. You punch us, we get sad." He then comically parodied the Left-leaning commentary that follows the sadness, but attributed the difference in reactions to "low self-esteem" on the Left. I agree with his observations, but disagree with his explanation of the cause.

I've seen people on the Left retreat from any civic conflict out of a multi-level discomfort with conflict itself: discomfort with physical tension, emotional tension, ideological debate, and the perceived spiritual gaps they experience between what they value as harmony and positivity in life, and the demands on a citizen in a democracy to develop the skills of advocacy, debate, and public discussion. However, the central paradox within democracy creates continuous tension between what appears to many people, particularly people whose psyches are uninitiated as mature souls, as irreconcilable opposites.

Democracy is the vibrant, oscillating dynamic between individual freedom and social justice, and it utterly depends on citizens' willingness to engage in this paradox out of love for democracy. Lewis Lapham states:

Democracy assumes conflict not only as the normal but also the necessary condition of its existence, the structure of the idea resembling a suspension bridge dependent upon the balance between countervailing forces. The project collapses unless the stresses oppose one another with more or less equal weight—unless enough people have enough courage to sustain the argument between the government and the governed, capital and labor, men and women, matter and mind.[124]

Courage is needed by people in the media to shift the entire industry so that it provides Americans with factual context, a range of viewpoints, and intelligent debate instead of bickering.

These three factors are not intended as exhaustive by any means, but do indicate systemic causes potentially eroding Americans' willingness to persist as active citizens in the democracy experiment.

WHAT DO YOU BELIEVE IS "HUMAN NATURE"?

It all comes down to how you answer this question: what do you believe constitutes "human nature"?

Libertarian ideology cleaves to the idea that human nature is based on self-interest. The rights of the individual for liberty, and the elimination of social justice as a goal, are ideas aligned with the core philosophy that human nature is primarily self-interested. Libertarians read Ayn Rand and use her philosophy for support because she developed an entire philosophical system called Objectivism, which is based on this fundamental conviction that the core of human nature is self-interest.[125]

If you also believe this, then you're right on time with an ever-growing influence in American politics and economics and can lend your voice to further dismantling the democratic ideal and systems of delivery.

If you do not believe this circumscribed view of human nature, then it is time for you to speak up for the democracy ideal. Every day that goes by without your voice enables greater dismantling of democracy.

Something has got to give. It is time to go to another level of development in America—not economic development—but moral, ethical, and spiritual development in the heart of our national culture. There is enough scientific evidence today to drastically change our ideas about what constitutes human nature. Frans de Waal, director of the Yerkes National Primate Research Center at Emory University, has spent thirty years researching components of "human nature" and presents some surprising findings. So also do neuroscientists studying our capacity for empathy and cooperation. For example, (1) systems of mirror neurons within the human brain trigger how we see ourselves in others, learn from others, and feel compassion for them; (2) the neuroplasticity of our brains indicates we can learn, grow and change at any age, and develop beyond the confines of outdated theories; and (3) Dr. Candace Pert's research on the human body's receptor sites demonstrated the biochemical basis of emotions and how body-mind molecular networks impact our health. It is time to understand that "human nature" is not set in stone, that it can include a multi-dimensional understanding that human beings are body, heart, mind, and spirit simultaneously, and that we are interconnected.

To the quantum physicist, we are "entangled," and this entanglement is being discovered in one scientific experiment after another as being more primary to life than time and space.[126]

In other words, a human being is not "atomistic," separated, and alienated from the whole, but is an integral part of the whole. We are, as a species, facing the evolutionary requirement[127] to see ourselves as simultaneously unique individuals and also as integral to the whole. This is our next level of development in America, and democracy is the ideal system to support this elevated understanding of the human being. We are learning how. We must continue in the democracy experiment.

The "atomistic" view of a human being is an Enlightenment view, and was a necessary reaction against the church-dominated view of humans as collectively doomed. That was then, and it served its important purpose in moving humans forward to honor individual rights as both ideal and in practice. This is now. Our mounting environmental and economic crises are forcing us to wake up to a different view of ourselves than an atomistic one, and to a different view of society than one based on social Darwinism.

It is long past time to move to a new understanding of humans as integral to an ecosystem of interrelationships, as "entangled" with each other and the natural world. The challenge is to hold the paradox of both individual rights and social justice simultaneously.

This needed shift is appalling to the libertarian. It would appall Ayn Rand, too. The philosophy of self-interest allows us to not be responsible for anyone else's circumstances, and to act as if all of our food, clothing, shelter, conveniences, and resources simply arrive unencumbered by social responsibility to anyone for anything, simply because we have paid for them.

Gary Weiss provides a useful insight regarding the appeal of Ayn Rand to Americans who may be losing heart for social justice:

> _Atlas_ and _Fountainhead_ made it easy to love individualism and no-government capitalism because it was a world of healthy, young heroes and repulsive villains. There were no inconvenient elderly defecating upon themselves in nursing homes. No paraplegic war veterans without means of support. No refugees from far-off lands with unmarketable skills. No KKK rallies. No exploitation of the poor. No rat-infested slums. No racial minorities. Poverty and unemployment are a distant, alien presence. The only member of the underclass Dagny encounters is a railroad hobo who turns out to be an Objectivist with a lead on Galt. There is nobody and nothing to interrupt the monotonous picture, nothing to upset the stereotypes, no migrant workers toiling for pennies. Rand, acting as God, made those people invisible while she whitened the hearts of American business. The only societal problem in the world of Atlas Shrugged is that government is mean to business and unfair to the wealthy.[128]

We have had enough of a debased view of human nature as only self-interested. It is out of date. Antiquated. It is time to get an upgrade for our view of human nature so that we can get past the bickering and "battles over a rattle," and get to the creative work of designing the types of social systems, business systems, community systems, and all resource systems that elevate the human community and all life on Earth.

DEMOCRACY IS NOT AN ECONOMIC SYSTEM

Democracy is not a synonym for capitalism, socialism, or communism. Democracy is not confined within any economic system. Democracy is a principle of the simultaneity of individual freedom and social justice. It is a living principle calling us to a larger life. It is breaking through cultures all over the world, such as Tunisia and Egypt, where people are stating, "I'm willing to die for freedom in my country," as people once said in an earlier time in America.

DEMOCRACY IS NOT SUBORDINATE
TO CAPITALISM

Capitalism is subordinate to democracy because capitalism has nearly run its course, given capitalism's insistence on dominating and controlling both nature and the majority of humanity. Democracy is the much larger canvas on which humanity must create anew and evolve, and also must discover new, life-sustaining economic systems.

Democracy does not require predatory capitalism to fund its life. On the contrary, from a position of democracy, we can envision beyond the out-of-date economics that offer only a false dichotomy of either capitalism or socialism, and open our minds and creative imaginations to economic systems that serve human life and creative ingenuity.

Why not? What cynical frameworks of human nature and economics are we married to that would drag down all creative possibilities for a new economy into the muck of the past?

If we wish to go forward in a truly new way in America, let's not be glib about it. Let's be alert and aware of two warnings—one recent and indirect, and one two hundred years old and direct.

The recent, indirect warning comes from the pages of a libertarian social researcher, Charles Murray. He assumes his view of human nature as self-interested is a given and is the correct view. Thus, his interpretations of social data in America all lead to rather grim conclusions, for which the dismantling of democratic policies and systems is the solution. Be aware of how and why libertarians offer the conclusions they offer.

Murray was co-author with Richard Herrnstein of the controversial book *The Bell Curve*,[129] and has recently written another book, *Coming Apart: The State of White America, 1960–2010*.[130] Much of his research has valuable data, which more Americans should understand, and Murray himself indicates sincere concern about the increasing divisions between economic classes and races in America. Yet, consider the following regarding his views of human nature and the reductionism applied to causality in social justice systems:

> *I am predicting that over the next few decades advances in evolutionary psychology are going to be conjoined with advances in genetic understanding, leading to a scientific consensus that goes something like this: There are genetic reasons, rooted in the mechanisms of human evolution, why little boys who grow up in neighborhoods without married fathers tend to reach adolescence not socialized to the norms of behavior that they will need to stay out of prison and to hold jobs. These same reasons explain why child abuse is, and always will be, concentrated among family structures in which the live-in male is not the married biological father. These same reasons explain why society's attempts to compensate for the lack of married biological fathers don't work and will never work.*[131]

Murray then offers several other points about human nature and behavior that he believes "the neuroscientists and geneticists will prove over the next few decades," and explains,

. . . I have entitled this section "Watching the Intellectual Founda-tions of the Welfare State Implode" to reflect my confidence that the more we learn about how human beings work at the deepest genetic and neural levels, the more that many age-old ways of thinking about human nature will be vindicated.[132]

Be aware of those who equate the "welfare state" with the democratic ideal of social justice, and therefore seek to convince you why America should divorce "justice for all" from "liberty for all." The phrase "welfare state" is inherently derogatory and a coded message for dividing groups of Americans against each other, rather than considering the systemic causes of social problems. The term "social justice" is an uplifting term, not a derogatory term, unless you have been conditioned to equate the two.

A two hundred-year-old, direct warning comes from Alexis de Tocqueville in his classic work, *Democracy in America:*

There is, indeed, a most dangerous passage in the history of a demo-cratic people. When the taste for physical gratifications among them has grown more rapidly than their education and their experience of free institutions, the time will come when men are carried away and lose all self-restraint at the sight of the new possessions they are about to obtain. In their intense and exclusive anxiety to make a fortune they lose sight of the close connection that exists between the private fortune of each and the prosperity of all.

It is not necessary to do violence to such a people in order to strip them of the rights they enjoy; they themselves willingly loosen their hold. The discharge of political duties appears to them to be a trouble-some impediment, which diverts them from their occupations and business. If they are required to elect representatives, to support the government by personal service, to meet on public business, they think they have no time, they cannot waste their precious hours in useless engagements; such idle amusements are unsuited to serious men who are engaged with the more important interests in life. These

people think they are following the principle of self interest, but the
idea they entertain of that principle is a very crude one; and the bet-
ter to look after what they call their own business, they neglect their
chief business, which is to remain their own masters.[133]

Let's heed these two warnings, one indirect and one direct, and get on
with bringing a new, elevated definition of a human being and a new era
of democracy's paradoxical ideal to America.

MATURING INTO THE SOUL IS REQUIRED

The future isn't going to be easy. But America has faced profound ethical
and moral crossings before, and can cross the turbulent river again with
our willingness to mature our personal soul and our nation's soul.

Democracy is best lived through and protected by emotionally mature,
initiated humans who consciously bear the paradoxical tension between
being unique individuals in freedom while simultaneously being in service to the greater life of the human community. It is not lived through nor
protected by people in the caterpillar stage. Neither major political party,
nor the Libertarian party, has a corner on the maturity required.

Nevertheless, people can grow. In fact, the nature of the human psyche
requires we grow and it presents us with challenges to force that growth.[134]
As a nation, we are being forced to grow. Circumstances both internal and
external to our national culture are forcing us as Americans to own up to
what we mean by "democracy," how many lives we're committed to killing,
including American soldiers' lives, in order to force "democracy" down
another nation's throat. It may sound obvious to state that people of any
political viewpoint can grow, mature, and change, but it wouldn't appear
that way given our current political climate.

Consider a comparison of two famous and powerful men. Each had a
very different way of facing responsibility for the impacts of their power
over the lives of millions of people. Each had a very different way of choosing to mature into the initiated soul, or not.

In the film *The Fog of War*, an elderly Robert McNamara, the Secretary of Defense who drove escalation of the Vietnam War, admits to his responsibility for countless deaths and horror, and states that society should see him as a war criminal. However late in life it happened, he finally dropped down to his knees in admission of his responsibility to the larger life of humanity, and died to his old self-definition as "right."

He no longer justified, defended, nor rationalized his actions during the war, but finally bore the moral burden of what it meant to the entire human community. His soul matured. He did not use the term "the Commons," but his demeanor and words indicated he knew he had violated it. He became humbled.

In contrast to McNamara is the behavior of Alan Greenspan after the economic crises of the sub-prime mortgage scandal erupted in the U.S. in 2008, and caused ripple crises globally. As Federal Reserve Chairman, Greenspan was the chief architect and promoter of the policies and systems that dismantled regulations, such as repeal of the Glass-Steagall Act in 1999, which encouraged predatory lending that led to the crises. Greenspan had opposed Congress' prior attempts in 2002 to close loopholes in derivatives trading, and had blocked other efforts at reform.[135]

When he came before the Congressional hearing in 2008, he admitted to finding a "flaw in the model" he had apparently believed was flawless, and stated "those of us who have looked to the self-interest of lending institutions to protect shareholders' equity, myself included, are in a state of shocked disbelief." This is hardly an admission of adult responsibility for the power he wielded over the lives of millions. It is a statement of an uninitiated person who blames others. Weiss gives us insight into the next stages of what occurred:

> The "flaw" speech made headlines around the world. It was almost universally interpreted as a repudiation of his free-market ideology, and to this day it is one of the seminal moments in the financial crisis. But as I studied his public comments, I came to realize that it wasn't quite the mea culpa that it was portrayed as being. The word

"doubletalk" came to mind. Yes, he admitted a "flaw." He used that word. Asked if he was wrong, he said "partially." But he backtracked almost as soon as those words left his mouth. Remarkably little attention was paid to his dissembling and backsliding on his personal, ideologically driven culpability.[136]

Greenspan's mentor was Ayn Rand. His ideology is the Objectivist philosophy of her writings, which values a certain approach to mental reasoning, based on individual self-interest as the only logical perception of "reality." No other versions of reality are valid, according to Objectivism.

Rand's philosophy matters to Americans for three major reasons: (1) Rand believed in democracy only for the wealthy—an oligarchy; (2) across decades, through the work of her adherents with economic power and political status, her philosophy has served to justify private interests that have been twisting our democracy toward an oligarchy and plutocracy, and claiming these distortions as "reality"; and (3) trends indicate increasing numbers of Americans are reading Rand's works, which portends some impact we have yet to understand.

My contention is that Rand did not become initiated into a larger life, but rather rationalized away the transformational demands on her psyche. I propose that, despite her many accomplishments and unique philosophical contributions, she did not mature into the soul required for our times today. She did not die to her cherished identity from the past, but rather stayed curiously aligned with many of the values she had developed as an adolescent.[137] Her traumatic youth in Russia at the time of the Bolshevik revolution when her family's survival was threatened shaped her contempt for socialist collectivism as "evil."[138] Consequently, she expressed contempt for any group-level dynamics. Her entire ideology became a "good versus evil" construction, the exact opposite of paradox. Her experience of Russian politics, frozen forever in time and then extrapolated to all societies across all time, shaped her views of the Commons as "meaningless"[139] and contributed to her view of capitalism as the carrier of freedom. She claimed, "Those who advocate laissez-faire capitalism are the only advocates of man's rights."[140]

Her philosophical views were rigorous and coherent, as far as they went within her "good versus evil" framework. In fairness, she did raise questions that deserve serious consideration for governing society ethically. But the questions only went so far, circumscribed as they were by her assumptions that most human beings are "parasites," living off of the achievements of a few creative individuals such as the protagonists in her novels. Her solution to the messy paradox of democracy's ideal was to vehemently reject all ethical obligations to others as delusional. Presto! The tension of the paradox is gone!

If you think Rand's influence today is minimal, think again. There are those in office right now who see many Americans as parasites, which is exactly why they seek to eliminate what they call "entitlements" for those so-called parasites. Their very attitudes reflect the uninitiated psyche of the self-serving, voracious caterpillar. We cannot afford to be ignorant about how the "good versus evil" construction of the uninitiated psyche within any one of us wreaks havoc on all of us.

When uninitiated people are in power, they threaten the "Commons" because they have no sense that it even exists. The "Commons" is simply denied. Poof! Barry Spector states, "A powerful man who remains a boy emotionally endangers the *polis*."[141] McNamara eventually matured from self-interested boy to self-reflective man, though it took nearly his entire life. Greenspan has not yet made that developmental transition.

Democracy needs protecting and defending, and it is best protected by emotionally mature, initiated humans who consciously recognize the difference between an initiated and an uninitiated person, and know how to stop the widespread bullying by the childish person in power.

It is necessary to consider whether people who use Rand's philosophy today in order to justify the dismantling of democracy are themselves seeking to avoid change and transformation into a larger life, and thereby avoid the inner death of cherished values that no longer make sense in our "entangled" world.

Any mature souls who know our undeniable "entanglement"—across any part of the political spectrum—need to unite together to stop the bullying of our democracy, and engage together in civic debate about how we will fulfill the paradoxical ideal of democracy.

One of the most important actions we must take to promote the civic debate needed to grow real democracy is to shift our own thinking and speaking about the challenges in America from a narrow, bickering either/ or construction—away from a "good versus evil" construction—to a systemic context that includes both the pros and the cons of an issue, both the benefits and the detriments of our offered solutions, both the long-term commitment to our democratic ideal of "liberty and justice for all," and the short-term practical steps that will help us move forward, even if such steps are incomplete and far from ideal. Robert Johnson encourages us to a larger life, "To transfer our energy from opposition to paradox is a very large leap in evolution."[142]

We must be willing to entertain the possibility that all people can change, that anyone can grow at any time, in direct contrast to the Randian and libertarian conviction that human nature is fixed and self-serving.

THE GREATER DREAM OF DEMOCRACY LIVES INSIDE ALL OF US

Today, as civic confusion swirls about us, it seems crucial to acknowledge the ancient root for *civic* is the same as that for *beloved* and *dear*. Will our beloved democracy endure in America even in its currently flawed form? Whether or not it does endure and mature to a deeper level may depend, perhaps entirely, on the ability of Americans to persist and persevere in this living experiment of participative governance.

NOTES

104 Jung, Carl. *Modern Man in Search of a Soul.* San Diego: Harcourt Brace, 1933, p. 184.

105 Meade, Michael. *The Water of Life: Initiation and the Tempering of the Soul.* Alaska: GreenFire Press, 2006, p. 326.

106 Johnson, Robert. *Owning Your Own Soul.* San Francisco: Harper, 1991.

107 Jung, Carl. *The Archetypes and the Collective Unconscious.* Princeton: Princeton University Press, 1969.

108 Hubbard, Barbara Marx. *Conscious Evolution: Awakening the Power of Our Social Potential.* Novato: New World Library, 1998.

109 Jung, Carl. *Aion: Researches into the Phenomenology of the Self.* Princeton: Princeton University Press, 1969.

110 Savage, Chris. "The Scandal of Michigan's Emergency Managers." *The Nation.* February 15, 2012.

111 Weiss, Gary. *Ayn Rand Nation: the Hidden Struggle for America's Soul.* New York: St. Martin's Press, 2012, p. 94.

112 Martin, Douglas. "David Nolan, 66, is Dead: Started Libertarian Party." *The New York Times.* November 22, 2010.

113 The preamble to the Libertarian Party platform. See: www.lp.org

114 Rushkoff, Douglas. *Life Inc.: How the World Became a Corporation and How to Take it Back.* New York: Random House, 2009.

115 Gonzales, Laurence. "No Margin for Error." *Adventure.* November 2004, pp. 54–58 and 87–90.

116 Alexander, Michelle. *The New Jim Crow—Mass Incarceration in the Age of Colorblindness.* New York: The New Press, 2010.

117 Weiss, Gary. op.cit. pp. 16-17. 2012.

118 Schor, Juliet. *Plenitude: The New Economies of True Wealth.* New York: Penguin Press, 2010. p. 106.

119 National Sleep Foundation. "Longer Work Days Leave Americans Nodding Off on the Job." March 2008. www.sleepfoundation.org

120 Schor, Juliet. *The Overworked American: The Unexpected Decline of Leisure.* San Francisco: HarperCollins, 1991.

121 Wikipedia, see: "United States incarceration rate." en.wikipedia.org/wiki/United_States_incarceration_rate

122 Lerner, Michael. *The Left Hand of God: Healing America's Political and Spiritual Crisis.* San Francisco: Harper, 2006, p. 51.

123 Streeck, Wolfgang. September–October 2011. "The Crisis of Democratic Capitalism." *New Left Review.* Vol. 71. www.newleftreview.org

124 Lapham, Lewis. "Ignorance of Things Past: Who Wins and Who Loses When We Forget American History." *Harper's.* May 2012, pp. 26–33 and 31.

125 Rand, Ayn. *Introduction to Objectivist Epistemology.* New York: Meridian, 1990.

126 Vedral, Vlatko. "Living in a Quantum World." *Scientific American.* June 2011, pp. 38–43.

127 Hubbard, Barbara Marx, op.cit.

128 Weiss, Gary, op. cit., p. 25.

129 Murray, Charles and Richard Herrnstein. *The Bell Curve: Intelligence and Class Structure in American Life.* New York: The Free Press, 1994.

130 Murray, Charles. *Coming Apart: The State of White America, 1960-2012.* New York: Crown Forum, 2012.

131 Ibid, p. 299.

132 Ibid, p. 300.

133 De Tocqueville, Alexis. *Democracy in America,* Vol. 2. New York: Vintage Classics, 1990, pp. 140–141.

134 Johnson, Robert, op. cit.

135 Weiss, Gary, op.cit., pp. 224–225.

136 Ibid, p. 227

137 Heller, Anne C. *Ayn Rand and the World She Made.* New York: Anchor Books, 2009.

138 Ibid.

139 Rand, Ayn. *Capitalism: The Unknown Ideal.* New York: Signet, 1967, p.12.

140 Rand, Ayn. *The Virtue of Selfishness.* New York: Signet, 1964, p. 117.

141 Spector, Barry. *Madness at the Gates of the City: The Myth of American Innocence.* Berkeley: Regent Press, 2010, p. 83.

142 Johnson, Robert, op. cit., p. 85.

CHAPTER SIX

DEFINING IDEOLOGIES WITH A CULTURAL COMPASS

By Benjamin "Nick" Colby

WE ARE LIVING in a Dickensian era—the best and the worst of times. On the one hand, the transforming culture of science and technology are making great strides in discovering what makes for a long and healthy life, while the emerging digital environment puts the world virtually at our fingertips.

But we are also living in an age of anxiety, one in which opportunities are narrowing. The public's trust in government, banks, and business is diminishing. Today, an almost-feudal society is developing and a new royalty of billionaires and cash-rich multimillionaires holds court at Bilderberg and Davos and in the boardrooms of major corporations around the world.

The wider the gap between this superclass and the rest of the world, the worse off ordinary people become. Great inequalities lead to symptoms of prolonged stress. The society we live in has been subverted and our culture has become ill.

When the culture of an entire society becomes sick, how do we know it? How do we feel? The symptoms vary according to the nature of that sickness. We may feel that life is harder, that somehow things aren't what they used to be. We fall into using maladaptive defense mechanisms. We are more anxious about things. We feel less secure. We become pessimistic about our chances for success. But even though we may experience some or all of these symptoms, it is hard to understand why. Some people blame themselves. Others create scapegoats and blame people around them. Still, others blame people in distant lands and support wars against them. In all these reactions, ideology plays a role.

A healthy culture is as necessary as the air we breathe. It is our language, our values, our attitudes, the very ambience of our lives. Yet bits and pieces of culture change without our taking notice. For instance, after the fall of the Roman Empire, Latin, which was spoken in Italy and many of its conquered territories, became what we call the Romance languages today. These include Italian, Spanish, Portuguese, French, and Romanian, all of which were once mere dialects of Latin that are now mutually unintelligible languages. Some aspects of culture change rapidly; others more slowly. Some are explicitly recognized; others are more insidious. Some are beneficial; others are pathological. But on what basis can we say that this or that aspect of culture is beneficial or pathological? The medical sciences make diagnoses and prescribe curative action for bodily pathology, but how can science deal with *cultural* pathology?

Anthropology, the one discipline that focuses on studying culture, rarely provides any basis for identifying or diagnosing a sick culture, much less prescribing a cure. But this is a problem only if we adhere to an old-fashioned view of culture as a spirit of the times, a zeitgeist that envelops us. A newer view of culture, one emerging from data in the neurological and biological sciences, gives us a better understanding of culture as both system and process—as something linked intimately to biological and ecological forces—residing in our brains and our bodies and shaped by our surroundings and our circumstances.

In daily life, the word culture has begun to take on something like this new usage, but without the science. We now explain the demise of Enron by its dishonest "culture" and the arrogance of Goldman Sachs by the exploitative "culture" of its executives. We talk about "culture wars" between political parties or between the Tea Party and Occupy movements.

This differs radically from the old anthropological view of cultural relativism, and that's a good thing. In the 1970s, graduate students and newly minted young faculty came to anthropology enthusiastic about postmodernism. They rejected the old view of culture in which we are its passive recipients, as if culture exists apart from our biology and our ecological context. But they retained the idea of cultural relativism, a morally and culturally non-judgmental view of an unfamiliar culture in the false belief that such a view is objective and hence scientific.

In effect, the postmodernists threw out the old cultural baby, but kept its bath water. Today, postmodernism is past its peak. Yet in anthropology little has come to take its place. So, in order to provide a useful understanding of the cultural conditions of our time—from which solutions to our problems can emerge—we must develop a new, more relevant anthropology.

Through a view of culture informed by findings in the social, cognitive, and neurological sciences, I propose a cultural compass that boils down policies, agendas, and ideologies to two simple matrices. One is for the biomaterial realm. The other is for the social realm. These two realms demonstrate how the presence or absence of the key cultural conditions— efficacy and diversity (for the biomaterial realm), and prosocial autonomy and affiliation (for the social realm)—explain something about the cultural health of the policies, agendas, and ideologies currently promoted by politicians, pundits, news commentators, and the wider media.

Whether our future will be one of well-being and cultural health or its opposite can be foretold by how elections turn on these basic values. In these times, the major differentiating value to watch for is *affiliation*. The quadrants of the cultural compass that measure affiliation—its presence or lack thereof, or even denial—are especially germane to our current political climate.

Before examining the cultural compass, there needs to be a general orientation. The first thing to notice should be the economics and politics of current culture, the two areas that are bringing the most malaise and misery to society today. Using our entirely new way of looking at culture as a dynamic within its natural and historic contexts, we must focus on these two areas, just as physicians focus on the core cancers in an afflicted body.

This new kind of approach to anthropology will aid in our political decisions and help us, as active cultural transformers, move toward a culture of health and well-being.

IDEOLOGIES AND THE NATURAL RIGHTS OF MAN

The Birth of a Nation

Ideologies are shaped largely by how people relate to each other as family members, community members, and national citizens. Some ideologies push agendas that run counter to widespread scientific findings. Others justify financial dealings in terms of nineteenth-century economics and a dubious morality. But some ideologies are in accord both with current science and with the ideas on which the founding of the United States was based.

Benjamin Franklin, Thomas Jefferson, James Madison, and the framers of the Constitution were among those responsible for establishing an early democracy through the Constitution and the Bill of Rights. As this vision was being shaped, influential writers like Thomas Paine galvanized colonists into supporting the call for independence from Britain and the need for a new form of government.

Those times involved a great ferment of political, philosophical, and religious ideas. It was the Age of Enlightenment. People began to speak of the natural rights of man, saying that there were certain human rights that were inalienable across all social and cultural differences. In speaking of the natural rights of man, the framers of the Constitution evinced an astute thesis for the times: that within every person there is a sense of justice which is part of man's basic nature, his "natural" endowment.

The Perennial Philosophy

If one goes back to major religious leaders, we find that they all express similar ideas about what is "natural." Most notably are the ethics, morality, and prescriptions of the three middle-eastern religions, all of which touched upon justice and basic human concerns. We can also go back further in time to Gautama Buddha, the founder of Buddhist traditions. He argued that thoughtful people did not need hierarchies or even laws, as long as they were perceptive and recognized the consequences of certain behaviors.

Aldous Huxley observed a deep similarity among these and other philosophies and religions—a natural perception of how people nurture their better natures. He called it the perennial philosophy.[143]

The Linkage of Ideologies to Narratives, World View and Science

How best might this inner wisdom of the natural man be brought out in people as they grow up and engage with the world? Since ancient times, it was done mostly with aphorisms, proverbs, and stories. That still holds true today, except we add to them the printing press, film, television, and the Internet. From various sources, both traditional and new, one can benefit from the wisdom of those who came before us. Stories, and the knowledge they bring, provide a code of thought and behavior. Such a code can be encapsulated in a philosophy of life and a politics that is suitable for stormy times. In fact, it can guide us in assessing the various ideologies being hawked today.

Ideologies are part of one's wider culture. They are humanity's way of responding to situations and environments that can lead to social betterment. But they also are subject to manipulation by individuals with special interests. When those individuals gain leverage through financial means, we can be led astray. We could even be faced with social collapse. Just as with our personal physical health, we must attend to our cultural health, at least if we are to have an impact on our society and community.

Ideologies, like the wider culture of which they are a part, can use the tools of technology and science to improve cultural well-being. But culture can also use technology to bring on cultural malaise. Culture can end up serving some (like the one percent) at the expense of others (the 99 percent). Today, an enormous wealth gap has grown between the power elite in the financial and corporate world on the one hand and everyone else on the other. Cultural dynamics are shaping society in ways that might be called a monetary feudalism. With billions of dollars at their beck and call, many among the ruling elite assume a sense of entitlement that places them and their power above the law and above the well-being of millions, if not billions of people in America and around the world.

Civil liberties are being eroded at an unprecedented speed, while perpetual war feeds upon itself. Private armies are used for military support while health and freedom are denied to many. There is money to build new prisons, but schools are deprived of funds.

Except for the Tea Party (supported largely by elements of the corporate sector), the Occupy Wall Street movement, and the Wisconsin demonstrators, there has been an incomprehensible lack of outrage about the agendas that have brought such egregious developments in our cultural systems. The privatization of profit has increased while investment risks are born by the public. The downsizing of government, the elimination of governmental regulatory control of corporate behavior (controls established for worker safety, consumer protection, public honesty, and fairness), and the subsidies and tax reductions that government gives to corporations have come about from the tremendous surge in the number of corporate lobbyists and the funding they command in Washington D.C. The enormous amount of financial support they provide to individuals in all three branches of government—branches that were originally expected to supply checks and balances among the legislative, judiciary, and administrative offices of government—have provided corporations with a controlling advantage.

The Economics

Much of the problem comes from an economic system that is dividing populations in America, Europe, and countries around the globe. For a comfortable living today, families require two income earners in order to enjoy a lifestyle that in the 1950s required only one income. So how did all this come about? What do we need to understand in order to reverse these trends? What do the latest scientific findings suggest?

To answer these questions, we first must deal with the stories, myths, and narratives that are pervasive in our culture. This includes what we see in the media as well as what we observe from our own direct experience. However, a moment's reflection will remind us that advertisers and the private ownership of most mainstream media would direct us away from considering the negative consequences of whatever ideas or products they are selling. It is time that we educate ourselves about the biases inherent in their narrative.

Our experiences can either support or weaken the ideologies we encounter. Every day, we are confronted with news and interpretations that reflect ideological biases. The forms are multiple: stories, short or long, informing or entertaining, and lifestyle vignettes or appeals to self-image. We run into these ideologically shaped bits and pieces while shopping, listening to political speeches, watching sporting events or movies, attending church, going to the theater, or traveling through cyberspace on the Internet. In our minds, we also construct story-like "recordings" of our own direct observations and experiences—a deeper and nuanced kind of story—a full-length continuing story that reflects what we have observed and absorbed over the years.

In effect, these stories are used to formulate a deep cultural grammar. Just as with language grammars (the syntax and semantics of the language we use), we also construct a much deeper grammar of our experiences. Through all these stories, we build culture by means of this cultural grammar. Like the grammar in our spoken language, our cultural grammar is an unconsciously developed "grammar" that exists at a sub-semantic level. Linguists call this "pragmatics." Though cognitive neurologists have a long way to go in discovering how cultural grammars work in our brains, we know that they come from both direct and indirect experiences. We are impacted by stories of every type, whether our own lived story or stories told through the public media. These stories and the grammars they employ need to be coherent at the deepest level of cognition and feeling. Ideologies are explicit ways of bringing all this together.

Ideally, the two grammars (language and culture) will mesh, but what if they don't? Often, we find a disjunction between what comes to us from media stories and our internal cultural grammar. If our direct experience and our media-shaped experiences clash, this lack of coherence creates interference in our underlying cultural grammars. It is in the nature of our brains and our inner culture to have a coherent view of what is happening around us. We need this coherence. However, if key values in our underlying pragmatics are in conflict, we experience mental discomfort. Just as nature abhors a vacuum, humans abhor the conflict of values within their inner culture.

Ideologies both mirror and influence changes in behavior and life style. These symbolic processes involve art, celebrations, science, and discoveries. They are crucial to extracting meaning from what we do so that we can be happy and enthusiastic about life, particularly in the face of a storm of anthropogenic disasters.

Psychological discomfort when the storm is upon us will require drastic cultural transitions unless we prepare ourselves beforehand. We need to be creative and encourage a blossoming of activity in the symbolic realm: art, science, the performing arts, and spiritual celebrations.

THREE REALMS

The Symbolic Realm is one of three realms of human concern, the other two being the Biomaterial and the Social Realm. The cultural systems in any society can be best understood if we distinguish these three realms because each one involves a different set of values for survival and resilience:

1. The Biomaterial Realm concerns our physical health, our natural and built environments, including living conditions, nutritional intake, and our economy.
2. The Social Realm concerns our social relations in family, neighborhood, community, political system, and national policies regarding other nations and peoples.

3. The Symbolic Realm concerns our language, literature, art, science, religion, philosophy, and other symbolic activities that are enhanced through language and mathematics.

The Biomaterial Realm

The most basic of the three realms, the Biomaterial, is represented by the physical work we do to sustain ourselves and earn a living, the physical environment in which we are engaged, and the resources we use. Much of our activity in this realm is represented abstractly through money and, inadequately, by economics.

The three realms of human concern in real life are inextricably interrelated in many ways. Well-being, happiness, and physical good health require attention to *all three* of these realms. They build upon each other. Yet, the *conditions* of well-being and happiness differ according to the realm being considered.

Levels of Happiness

Happiness depends upon where you are at different levels of needs. Obviously, the most crucial need is for adequate food, water, clothing, shelter, and safety. When any of these needs are seriously lacking, happiness is defined as satisfying those needs. Essentially, these needs are of the biomaterial realm. But once those basic needs are fulfilled, happiness is defined by well-being in the other two realms, social and symbolic.

The Need for Culturally Embedded Economics

If we fail to link economics, a biomaterial concern, to the wider picture— one that includes the other two realms (social and symbolic), difficulties will invariably arise. If we do not include broader aspects of human concern in economic theory and thought, economics has failed us. As expressed by anthropological economist Karl Polanyi, financial markets must not be viewed as being independent from the rest of culture. Markets must be "embedded" in non-economic social processes if we are to avoid depression, widespread poverty, and cultural malaise. This is a lesson rarely considered in America or the European Union. Greece and many other countries have to undergo austerity because of banking operations created by the movers and shakers of the financial world. This exemplifies what can happen when economists show no concern for overall well-being in society (the other two realms). We saw the same process applied by the International Monetary Fund (IMF) in third-world countries, but the practice even goes back to colonial times and further.

Private Special Interests and Government Should Not Mix if Corruption of Government Is to Be Avoided

In order to embed economics into culture, governments should not allow private interests to commandeer the financial system of a country. This tendency for private interest to ride roughshod over the public welfare has a long history. During the time of the American Revolution, Amschel Rothschild, banker for William of Hanau, who arranged with the British to send a Hessian mercenary army to fight against the colonists in the American Revolution, was the founder of a family dynasty with five sons. One son remained with the father in Frankfurt and the other four were each sent to a major financial city of Europe: Vienna, Paris, Naples, and London. Nathan Rothschild was the son who went to London. He started with three million pounds from his father and embarked upon the economic machinations that brought him to the top of the financial pinnacle. One example attributed to him during the Napoleonic war was his spread of a well-timed rumor that Wellington had lost to Napoleon when in fact Nathan had advanced knowledge of Wellington's victory. The plunge in the stock market enabled Nathan to pick up investments at pennies to the pound. Nathan once said, "I care not what puppet is placed upon the throne of England to rule the Empire on which the sun never sets. The man who controls Britain's money supply controls the British Empire, and I control the British money supply."[144]

From the very beginning, the Rothschild dynasty was involved with financing military affairs for governments, much of which was kept secret. When the U.S. refused to go along with one of the Rothschild American ventures after the American Revolution, Nathan threatened war, and sure enough, we had the war of 1812, when British troops burned the White House and the Capitol. The current system in the U.S. follows that tradition of private bankers influencing the policies and affairs of national governments for their own financial gain. As Ellen Brown has detailed, "We and our money system are currently caught in a privatized and deceptive web of banking institutions that have drained public money to line the pockets of the elite."[145]

Brown describes how Ponzi financing was a key contributor to the precipitous 2008 stock market drop in America. Yet even though the drop was due to the predatory financing of large banks and financial companies, causing the stocks of those companies to plunge, the salaries and other forms of compensation for the top executives of those very same companies grew even larger.

Most American banks continued to operate as before, even after receiving large bailouts through the Federal Reserve (a private, not a government, body in spite of the word "federal"). But this largess scarcely trickled down to ordinary people, the 99 percent, in the current rhetoric of the Occupy Wall Street movement.

THE STAGNATION OF WAGES OVER THE PAST THIRTY-FIVE YEARS

Because the two principles—the need to embed economics in other sociocultural phenomena and the need to eschew private control of a country's currency—have been violated, corporations were able to keep wages low. Profits went to the executive officers (and some to stock holders) rather than employees. With the stock market drop of 2008, many wage earners lost their jobs altogether. Over the long term and since the Reagan administration, workers' unions have been weakened and the corporate world has become gigantic in its political influence. With the recent help of the

Supreme Court ruling (Citizens United v. the Federal Election Commission), which allows corporations to give unlimited financial support to corporate-favored politicians, the way is now clear for deep levels of corruption in all branches and levels of government.

PIERCING THE VEIL OF SECRECY

Why did so many Americans go along with the private interests of the power elite who were serving themselves, the military industrial complex, the interests of oil companies, coal companies, and others?

The first order of business should be to investigate the actions of office holders. That means going beyond what the candidates *say* and investigating what they *do*. We also must be alert to time-delay corruption via the revolving door, where politicians move from government regulation of corporations to high paying jobs within those very same corporations, often as lobbyists. So we need to track the tax breaks and subsidies for large corporations that politicians vote for. We also need to keep track of the energy interests that are seeking to discredit science, particularly through funding political campaigns and supporting so called "think tanks" supported by special energy interests.[146] In short, we need to monitor the integrity of politicians through research provided by voting citizens. When politicians play with the truth and use rhetoric to hide less than honorable motives, one has to redouble efforts to discover and understand the special interests they serve and what they are hiding from the majority of their constituents.

THE INTERNET DEVELOPS RHETORICAL SKILLS, WHICH INCLUDE LIE DETECTION

Parsing out ideological implications of what you hear and see over mainstream media requires an ability to separate the chaff of propaganda from the grain of truth. Here is where the Internet provides a valuable function. Through the Internet, there is a whole new world of science, technology, and art, and a wealth of information for the inquiring voter. But we need to develop techniques for sifting through it for accuracy. In short, we need evidence-based statements and not simply opinions, puffery, and attacks on character. We need criticism of people's statements and actions.

Blogs and comments to blogs can run the gamut from added information, contrary information, and unsupported opinions to misinformed ideas. An even more intense process occurs through Internet forums on a topic. To get through this thicket of competing rhetoric and varying quality requires an active search for accuracy of information and smart interpretive rhetoric. In this manner, the Internet goes beyond simply providing information. It can expand our minds and make us more critical if we develop the skills to seek out accuracy. Many among the younger generation have developed these skills quite well.

In contrast to a wide range of information, interpretation, and discussion available on the Internet, mainstream media (television and much printed matter) are an impoverished alternative. One-way statements largely in keeping with concerns of the power elite through their ownership and advertising revenue typify the mainstream. Aside from genuinely public supported radio and TV, the mainstream is distinctly slanted by various flavors of conservative ideas that serve special interests.

The Internet opportunity that invites people to comment on an article just posted presents a new model for thinking about news and opinions. This is an exercise in rhetoric, in learning what to look for or where to check claims being made about some subject, as well as how to judge those claims and determine how well the evidence supports them. How do we judge the competence of writers on politics and current events and the posted reactions to them? People are becoming more careful in deciding on the cogency of comments and suggestions, detecting emotional, irrational, and groundless reactions, which are often revealed by scurrilous language and non-sequiturs.

There is a related benefit to Internet usage. Through exposure to different ways of thinking, one builds up an elaborate coding of world events and opinions that widen perspective while improving thought and expression. Young and old alike have a new educational tool that provides equal opportunity for anyone who has online access, regardless of formal education.

However, a deeper kind of understanding is necessary to put those skills to best effect. One must become his own cultural analyst, anthropologist, sociologist, or investigative journalist, regardless of prior background. It requires a critical but open mind.

EMBEDDED ECONOMICS AGAIN

Context is critical. To reiterate economic anthropologist Karl Polanyi's point, economics must be contextualized in the widest cultural spectrum. As an academic field, economics needs to be culturally embedded in the three realms of cultural concern: Biomaterial, Social, and Symbolic. You can't keep money separate from everything else without creating social imbalances and inequalities. Moreover, markets cannot be self-adjusting by themselves because they are affected by the underlying sociality and materiality of life. Humans are social beings, not just faceless sources of economic exploitation and bailouts or "self-satisfying entities."

HUMANS ARE SOCIAL BEINGS

Can anyone seriously dispute the fact that we are social beings first and foremost? Why else would humans have developed language? Language is social "technology." We use it to communicate with our fellows, families, and communities, and much of this is economic in nature. There are social aspects to trade relations like gift giving and ritual donations that require language and all its underpinnings. All these interactions involve a necessary connection between our language grammars and our deeper-level cultural grammars. It was the development of language that gave our species such an advantage in evolution.

CONDITIONS OF SELECTIVE ADVANTAGE

As anthropologists and biologists often ask, what are the conditions that give a selective advantage to a person or group over the course of both cultural and biological evolution? It turns out that the three-realm approach is more than a simple classification of cultural phenomena. This approach yields realm-specific conditions of adaptive potential that provides a wide spectrum answer. Let's begin by looking at the Biomaterial Realm. The two conditions of adaptive potential for that realm are efficacy and diversity.

Efficacy

If there is one universally agreed-upon condition for success in natural selection—virtually synonymous with success—it is efficacy in responding to your environment, whether that environment is natural or social.

Diversity

But what happens when environments change? Some organisms can be so closely adapted to a particular set of circumstances that change might wipe out the organism. So efficacy is not sufficient in itself. There needs to be resilience, the ability to adjust to change and adversity. If you have experienced a greatly varied environment and have learned to adjust to those variations, you have developed a degree of resilience. Having a diversity of repertoire, of skills, of ways of doing things, comes not from simply learning new skills but also to adjusting to changing situations early on. Actually, it is common sense and comes straight out of the principles of natural selection in their most elemental form.

If you have a diversity of skills and a basic openness to diversity, you have more flexibility. You are more likely to survive through major changes in your social ecology as well as in the natural world. At the basic level of biomaterial existence, efficacy and diversity are the two primary conditions that will help you survive. This is illustrated in the diagram below where the two conditions, efficacy and diversity, are listed as high (plus sign) or low (minus sign), yielding a four-fold survival map characterizing (in three of the four spaces) people and groups who fall outside the double plus space. The double plus space itself is where the greatest success is likely to be found during times of extended adversity.

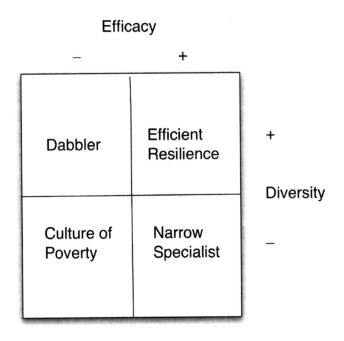

Efficacy

Figure 1: Conditions of Adaptive Potential in the Biomaterial Realm

Looking at each of the quadrants of the Biomaterial Realm of culture, we see the highest condition of adaptive potential to be in the double plus quadrant. High efficacy and high diversity together bring resilience in the face of change.

Diagonally, down to the lower left quadrant, is the double minus, meaning low in efficacy and low in openness to diversity. This condition was well described by anthropologist Oscar Lewis in his studies of slum life in Mexico and Puerto Rico. He developed the idea of a culture of poverty, people who could not make it for lack of schooling, resources, and other sociocultural disadvantages. But Lewis did not restrict his study to individuals who temporarily were out of luck and money. He studied generations of families where people were born into poverty and grew up in the same impoverished environment—what we might call a self-perpetuating culture.

LACK OF DEVELOPMENT

How does low efficacy and low diversity come about? Much of it depends upon the environment of your younger years. The deepest level begins with early development. Long before Gerald Edelman proposed his theory of neural Darwinism,[147] Canadian psychologist Donald Hebb[148] and Donald Forgays[149] at the University of Vermont showed that animals are better at problem solving if they have grown up in a rich environment containing objects they could play with. Perhaps Hebb's finding was no accident. As a child, Hebb was taught by his mother, who used anthropologist Maria Montessori's techniques where a rich variety of materials, most of them "autotelic" or self-teaching, provided a challenging and stimulating environment.

USE IT OR LOSE IT

A later research group showed that giving rats objects to play with affected their production of neurotransmitters and resulted in greater brain weight and dendritic branching.[150] Edelman's theory and new studies continue to validate this "use it or lose it" finding with respect to humans as well as animals. In childhood development, the diversity and quality of early exposure to other humans and the environment directly link to the development of intelligence. Mental deficiency can result from severe deprivation of normal diversity experiences.[151]

This need for stimulation continues into adulthood. Indeed, one of the worst punishments or torture is to deprive a prisoner of a stimulating environment through solitary confinement. To increase diversity of repertoire, one must be open to learning new cultural patterns. Some people have a high need for novelty, which usually means an open mind that facilitates the learning of diverse patterns. Whitbourne found that openness to diversity predicted a positive response to changes in family life and work.[152] Further, it stands to reason that seeing and doing many different things will result in the retention of a diversity of cultural patterns.

Where once the brain was thought to have developed entirely through genetic control, we now know that culture and environmental experiences alter the very structure of the brain itself. This is especially true of the cerebral cortex, where experiences—even before birth and on through life—shape this structure.[153]

Since both efficacy and diversity concern matters of immediate survival, we can speak of them as basic survival conditions. When individuals find themselves with high adaptive potential in the Biomaterial Realm, they are likely to be more contented and more optimistic about their ability to respond to new circumstances.

A QUICKENED PACE OF EVOLUTION VERSUS CONSERVATISM

Adaptive potential goes beyond a comfortable adjustment to one's niche. The insurance provided by openness to diversity and innovation, combined with efficacy, makes for evolutionary success. This is not to deny the value of traditions passed on from one generation to the next. Through most of human history the maintenance of traditional ways has had its advantages in the traditional accumulation and preservation of past wisdom. But today we advance faster and respond more readily to rapid changes. So openness to diversity takes on greater importance than ever before. Now we are afforded the tremendous advantage that the scientific method gives us, which includes the rapid communication of scientific findings throughout the world's scientific community.

When economists take on a conservative view, one wonders if it is due to their inability or their unwillingness to be open to changing experiences, or whether it's because of their failure to embed their work in a wider scheme of things, as Polanyi emphasized, work that goes beyond the mere material to include the Social and Symbolic Realms as well.[154]

ADAPTIVE POTENTIAL IN THE SOCIAL REALM

We now move from the Biomaterial to the Social Realm of culture. That realm includes political ideologies. Here we need a scientific approach where different ideologies can be assessed as they appear on a continuum, from culturally healthy to culturally pathological. But it's not just a matter of personal attributes. It also is a matter surroundings and circumstances. Situations of long-term stress and fear can have a devastating effect on personal psychology, which, when multiplied throughout a society, can deeply affect the shared culture of that society.

For generations, since the end of World War II, people have lived under the threat of nuclear annihilation. They have lived through almost continual warfare abroad and have fears that have been exacerbated and played upon by the American response to 9/11. Increased fear, stress, and psychological defense mechanisms have infused the major cultural systems of society. Airport searches have become a constant part of air travel, and surveillance of citizens has greatly increased. There are signs that the government seeks to patrol American skies with drones as well. Obviously, these measures have contributed to a long-term increase in stress.

Many people build a hard outer shell for protection from stress, but not necessarily from the actual events that produce that stress. People lacking sufficient diversity of abilities and openness to diversity are at a disadvantage and are likely to resist the very thought of change, even when such a change might make things easier for them in the long run.

We need a scientific approach that can cut through all the confusions, hot buttons, emotionalities, dispositions, and political agendas in order to diminish stress and maximize our cultural well-being. So, how do we maximize our cultural well-being in the Social Realm? What is the pathway to it? We start our journey with an understanding of a key social science concept: social inequality.

It turns out that social inequality links to virtually every major social index that measures cultural health. A high amount of inequality is a symptom of an unhealthy sociocultural system. We know this from numerous studies, including a summarizing study of the thirty-nine richest nations compared to each other on the basis of their respective negative social indicators.[155] In that study, America is at the very bottom of the thirty-nine richest nations. Unlike the higher level of sociocultural health that the U.S. enjoyed in the late 1950s through the early 1970s, it is now the most dysfunctional. In contrast, Japan (prior to the Fukushima national disaster), the Scandinavian countries, and some European nations were at the top or upper middle of the list. Their social indicators point to healthier societies. What are those indicators? Wilkinson and Pickett made up a list of measurable indicators that would diminish well-being in any society:

> *Low level of trust*
> *Mental illness (including drug and alcohol addiction)*
> *Lower life expectancy and high infant mortality*
> *Obesity*
> *Low educational performance in children*
> *High Teenage births*
> *High homicides*
> *High imprisonment rates*
> *Low social mobility (not available for U.S. states)*

Wilkinson and Pickett, however, did not rest with an intuitive judgment. They went beyond that to statistically validate the list used in their analyses of inequality.[156] They found that "the higher the score of the factors listed in the above Index of Health and Social Problems, the worse things are."[157]

Trust

Trust, the indicator at the top of their list, is an overarching value for all three realms of human concern: Biomaterial, Sociopolitical, and Symbolic.

Trust is needed in trade, food consumption, and finance in the Biomaterial Realm. It is needed in social relationships and politics in the Social Realm. Finally, in the Symbolic Realm, trust is integral to science, while authenticity—closely related to trust—is essential to art.

The low level of trust in the U.S. is typified by Senator James Inhofe of Oklahoma, who argues vehemently that global warming is a hoax. He is evidencing a myopic mistrust of the one area of greatest integrity in the world today, science. So important is trust and truth in science, and so rare are the cases where they are violated, that when trust and honesty *are* violated, major attention is given to those violations in the journal *Science* and in mainstream public newspapers and magazines.[158] When Inhofe and the Republican members of congress voted to register their disbelief in the process of global warming, we entered a sorry state indeed. Such posturing indicates either a science illiteracy that is dangerous to the nation, or it means lack of integrity in a political environment riddled with corruption by the fuel industry. Further, it suggests that global warming has joined evolution, abortion, and gay marriage as another hot button trigger for many on the religious right. It flies in the face of rational thinking. If all we were talking about was whether evolution or the Biblical creation story was true, there would not be a catastrophic outcome if either side were to prevail. But there *is* a catastrophic outcome involved in the global warming scenario. The fact that trust in the work of scientists is so lacking on the part of the public suggests how the public's ability to understand has been impacted by both a lack of education and continual bombardment from the airwaves and newspapers of biased publications financed by the oil industry and other corporate interests. This suggests a very deep dysfunction within American democracy today.

Anxiety

High anxiety often indicates a low level of trust, cultural health, and well-being. Wilkinson and Pickett cite a study by psychologist Jean Twenge, who tracked anxiety levels among college students from 1952 to

1993. She found that by the late 1980s, American children on average were more anxious than child psychiatric patients in the 1950s.[159] A similar rise in anxiety was found in other countries. In the last quarter of the century, however, social inequality added further to U.S. decline in social indicators, sending the U.S. considerably below the thirty-eight other rich countries in the Wilkinson and Pickett study.

How could the decline in U.S. sociocultural health have happened so precipitously? Here is what Wilkinson and Pickett have to say:

> As greater inequality increases status competition and social evaluative threat, egos have to be propped up by self-promoting and self-enhancing strategies. Modesty easily becomes a casualty of inequality: we become outwardly tougher and harder in the face of greater exposure to social evaluation anxieties, but inwardly—as the literature on narcissism suggests—probably more vulnerable, less able to take criticism, less good at personal relationships and less able to recognize our own faults.[160]

What seems to be at work here is a positive feedback loop, where the adaptive potential of Americans and other populations has seriously decreased.

While inequality is one cause of anxiety, there are other causes, namely social persecution for being different from the mold. Whether due to skin color, ethnicity, sexuality, education, or politics, an unhealthy society will scapegoat those who don't conform to whatever particulars the dominant culture demands. In extreme cases the government of such a society is called "totalitarian."

Consider the history of the last half of the twentieth century, with the perceived threat of communism. From 1950 to 1954, we endured Joseph McCarthy's false accusations of communist sympathizers and spies among liberal Americans. That was followed by the wars putatively fought to stop the spread of communism, with mandatory conscription up until 1973. Next, came the Nixon Watergate scandal in the 1970s, resulting in a serious loss of trust in government. Currently, the far right ideology would require that all of society agree with their positions on abortion and gay rights. One might see how the times could contribute to an increase in anxiety as a result of these totalitarian tendencies. Why are these tendencies toward totalitarian government so pervasive in this time of worsening economic conditions and continuing war? Well, that's just it. When people are most stressed, they are inclined to accept authoritarianism, and in more extreme situations, they might accept a totalitarian government. The authoritarian personality, a long studied syndrome, advocates hierarchy and promotes inequality, both in social and economic differences.[161]

A GRID MODEL OF SOCIAL MODALITIES AND POLITICAL IDEOLOGIES

The social inequality correlations are robust. But there is more. We can go further with a different measure of sociocultural health, one based not on the usual social indicators but on interviews and questionnaires.[162] This involves a direct measure of adaptive potential within individuals and societies. High adaptive potential indicates high well-being.[163]

The two key conditions of well-being in the social realm are affiliation and pro-social autonomy.

We can divide each of the two conditions into high (positive) and low (negative) levels. As in the previous table, this allows the creation of a fourfold table with each space or quadrant representing a combined value for each of the two social realm conditions. Each quadrant represents a distinct *modality* of social relations, as shown in Figure 2 below.

The modalities of social relations can be thought of as competitive, paternalistic, egalitarian, or hierarchical. The latter, hierarchical, is motivated by positions of command and obedience, or high status and low status levels. A theory of adaptive potential in the social realm is based on these four basic types, as shown in the diagram.

The quadrants of the social realm reflect relationships between people. In Guatemala, where I did field work, the relations between Indians and

"Ladinos" the Spanish speaking non-Indians, tended to sort out into three of the above categories: competitive, egalitarian, and paternalistic.[164] Later, with the invasion of counterinsurgency soldiers of the authoritarian Guatamalan government, the fourth quadrant, hierarchical, could be added to the modalities. As one might expect, the counterinsurgency, led by officers trained at Fort Benning, Georgia, involved great misery for the local population, who were forced into patrolling citizen groups to locate farmers in the area who might be sympathetic to a handful of guerrillas (some of whom were formerly in the military of the democratic government that was overthrown to establish a dictatorship).

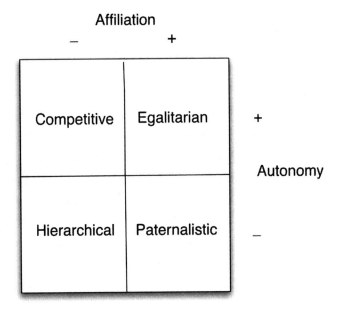

Figure 2: Four Basic Types of Social Modalities

If a person or an entire society scores as double plus (high affiliation and high pro-social autonomy), it signifies a condition of high sociocultural well-being. This condition can be characterized as an egalitarian situation, a reverse of the condition of inequality used by Wilkinson and Pickett in their work. Correspondingly, equality is associated with beneficial social indicators. So, equality's location in the double plus quadrant (high affiliation and high pro-social autonomy) is associated with many scientific studies over the last several decades that indicate sociocultural health.

The quadrant with high autonomy but low affiliation (i.e., an emphasis on individualism in a society but without social assistance for those in need, and without a focus on community or altruistic behavior) would, in theory, have to score lower in adaptive potential than in the double plus quadrant of egalitarianism because it has only a single plus, the one for autonomy. With low affiliation, the modality for that position is a competitive modality.

Moving to the lower right-hand quadrant, we have the diametric opposite of a competitive modality, low in prosocial autonomy but high in affiliation. I would describe it as a paternalistic system where the focus is on social assistance, but through governance over individual members who lack autonomy and are unable to input their own concerns about decisions by government. This condition of social relations characterizes a parent-child relationship and one among three kinds of relationships between ethnic groups where one group has a lower status than the other.[165] Affection is shown toward the different groups, but governance is rarely open to the lower-status groups.

Finally, in the lower left quadrant is the hierarchical modality, which emphasizes inequalities and status differences with a lack (minus value) of both autonomy and affiliation. As a double negative this modality strongly inhibits well-being, though it may have advantages in wartime or under siege when people are likely to submit to a more hierarchical governing system.[166]

Let's return to the top right quadrant, the egalitarian modality. With a long build up of an altruistic value system already in place, spontaneous altruism just happens. In an environment where people support one another, acts of altruism are often not the result of weighing and considering. They are spontaneous, involving quick assessments and spontaneous actions.

The chances and frequency of altruism and acts of kindness increase in a person who has grown up in a nurturing and secure home base. The nature of the social realm in one's life—its conditions and history—provides a solid foundation for altruistic actions and for caring, socially responsible actions.

When a society is high in affiliation and prosocial autonomy, people respect other people's individuality and autonomy, but also are favorably disposed to help as needed. But what happens to a group invaded by one or more "freeloaders" or argumentative types who do not reciprocate favors? To keep the group in a positive social modality, freeloaders and disrupters are excluded or punished. Altruistic punishment, that is, punishment by altruists of freeloaders and those who take unfair advantage of harmonious, democratic, or egalitarian social arrangements, is rewarded internally. That is, altruists get a sense of pleasure through actions that support the values of their group. Especially strong is the sense of fairness. Not allowing freeloaders to get away with taking advantage of the generosity of others without any reciprocal return of favors is a deeply felt sanction. Feeling good internally may be one motivation for whistle blowers when they see underhanded practices at work. However, it takes a certain tough-mindedness to take the risk they do when the social system has been corrupted. In a sick society, whistle blowers are often punished by corrupt governments instead of rewarded, as they would be in a society where government looks out for the well-being of its citizens.

Generally, being alert to moral wrongdoers provides an antidote to selfishness, immaturity, and unfairness in situations where cooperation and trust are important to people's well-being. When a person breaches those expectations with selfish, if not downright mean behavior, a healthy democracy enforces sanctions. But in an unhealthy environment, those sanctions bifurcate into two tiers. One for the power elite who are free from being prosecuted for wrong-doing, and the other for ordinary citizens who are not.

We can also approach the conditions for adaptive potential in the social realm from a developmental perspective, starting with the conditions that give newborns a healthy start in life. What are their needs as they enter this world? Infants are surrounded by family members who hold, carry, and care for them. Breast milk strengthens the bond between a newborn and the mother. Bodily smells and touch from other family members nurture a baby's life. What happens when that bonding process fails to take place?

It took until the mid-twentieth century before extreme cases of infant neglect woke people up to how sensitive babies and children are to bonding, i.e., to a caring, nurturing environment that fosters bonding.[167] In extreme cases, children confined in the most neglectful orphanages and child-care institutions developed marasmus—a loss of interest in any kind of environmental stimulus, which includes extreme lethargy, muscular flabbiness, retardation of mental growth, poor body reflexes, and sometimes death.[168] The lack of a nurturing environment is not confined to institutions. It can happen in dysfunctional nuclear families as well. In the 1940s, some mothers followed the advice of behaviorist psychologists who cautioned against picking up their babies when they cried for fear of spoiling them. The anthropologist Ashley Montagu included early orphanage studies and later more informed ones in a compendium of research he assembled to underline the importance of caring for and touching the developing infant.

The prolongation of infancy is a distinctive human evolutionary development, which, as Montagu explained, places special emphasis on touching and holding babies as a continuation of the gestative process outside the womb. Within the womb, the child is "enclosed and intimately bounded by the supporting, embracing walls of the uterus. This is a comforting and reassuring experience." But after the infant leaves this environment, close contact with the mother and being carried around, rocked, touched, and embraced by warm human beings is important.[169]

The British psychologist, John Bowlby, influenced by the early ethological literature on how animals bonded with their parents, developed a theory describing how small children attach to their parents, particularly the mother. Studies he conducted with Mary Ainsworth, an American developmental psychologist, show that the particular type of attachment a child develops can influence all close relationships throughout the child's future life.[170]

Attachment studies have shown that nurturance done correctly provides a child with a secure base, a sense of being loved, and the ability to love in turn. Providing a secure base will also build up independence and autonomy.

CONDITIONS FOR ALTRUISM

Virtually by definition, altruism assumes autonomy between the giver and receiver of an altruistic act. If there were no autonomy, if the relationship were a dominance/dependency one in either direction, the relationship would not be genuinely altruistic. A degree of freedom from dependency in a social group is a precondition for true altruism.

Often, altruism means going to some inconvenience for the self to provide help for someone else. If that someone else is a boss in a business, then one may not always be altruistic, but may be simply acting out one's duties as an employee. Relationships between parents and children aside, altruistic behavior must be freely given, without special interests or strings attached. The motivation of affiliation in a person's life—instead of coercion, command, and obedience—means that she gives helping behavior out of affection or out of values that have developed in a world that encourages empathy, sympathy, affiliation, fairness, and trust. In such a world, values of compassion develop and become part of one's "second nature."

There are also many trivial examples that add up to a happy day. Consider the time you were driving your car in a difficult traffic situation and another driver who had the legal right of way sized up the situation and motioned with her hand to yield her right of way and help you out of the problem. There are lots of other situations where you might have an inter-change with a complete stranger. Asking directions is a good illustration. If people know the area, they will usually go to some length to provide details about landmarks and such. Of course there are always exceptions, but smiles and acts of kindness are usually the rule rather than the exception in healthy societies during normal times.

SOCIAL SUPPORT

Social support among friends can be tremendously helpful to physical health as well as general well-being. It happens all the time. Numerous studies show that people with high social support get well sooner and get sick less frequently. It is also associated with longer life. And, by adding the broader concept, affiliation (i.e., the social support that involves warm and intimate relationships with family and friends), one could expect increased health and longevity.

Good social support, of course, depends on how well a person gets along with other people. Is the person in question expressive of her good feelings and attitude toward people? Is she happy for other people who have good fortune? Does she enjoy good company? Naturally, the very attributes in a person that make for good social harmony are likely to be attractive to others who participate socially with such a person. Getting along well with people and having an active social network enhances healthy emotions, empathy, and sensitivity.

However, in a society riven with class distinctions, with great inequality and lacking in universally good education there are likely to be fewer acts of kindness and less social support.

Mapping Ideologies on the Modalities Grid

Figure 3 below classifies some of the different kinds of ideologies that fit into the 4-space grid according to whether the ideology emphasizes affiliation, autonomy, or both (and their opposites).

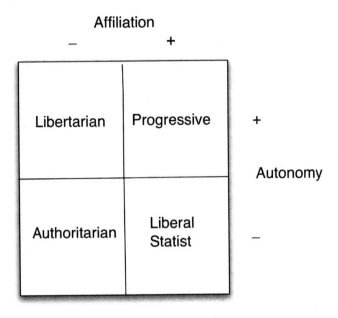

Figure 3: Ideologies of the Social Realm Quadrants

The progressive ideologies fit best into the egalitarian modality, values that promote freedom and protection under the law, the usual emphasis on *habeas corpus*, the requirement of search warrants, the protection of civil liberties, and the right to trial by jury. This approach also focuses on providing equal education, health care, and provisions for the poor, the handicapped, the sick, and the elderly.

Libertarian ideologies fit best into the competitive quadrant. Although the libertarian emphasis on autonomy varies, some advocates of this ideology vigorously defend the right for others to be autonomous. Others appear to stress autonomy for themselves rather than equally for everyone. In both cases, libertarians minimize community obligations.

Since the focus of this book is on libertarian ideology and its various "flavors," one might wish to go beyond varieties of libertarianism, to explore varieties of ideologies that occupy the two contiguous modalities: egalitarianism and authoritarianism. Egalitarianism is the logical domain of progressive ideologies. Authoritarian ideologies would fit in the hierarchical square. The double minus authoritarian ideologies are characterized by an absence of civil liberties, in contrast to the double plus progressive ideologies where civil liberties are emphasized.

One interesting approach is the type of anarchism advocated by the linguist Noam Chomsky, and perhaps a slightly different kind proposed by anthropologist David Graeber.[171] Chomsky emphasizes the idea of organic communities, which I would interpret to mean the full spectrum—i.e., all three realms of culture: Material (including biological), Social, and Symbolic. Chomsky also lists participatory action and the importance of community. Graeber does not always invoke a clear picture of anarchism, sometimes describing it as libertarianism but "with community." In both men's descriptions, however, anarchism would be closer to a double plus in the social realm than to libertarianism, which has only one plus—autonomy. A double plus is what I have labeled as egalitarianism in the cultural compass. However anarchism, particularly as Chomsky sees it, places major emphasis on a non-dominating social structure. That means avoiding hierarchy (except in special cases), which is a double minus.

In the U.S., where the support of community and social services have diminished substantially, one wonders whether those functions might be better served by local governments as opposed to national government. However, local governance has obvious limitations. As climate change takes a yet greater toll, entire states and regions may be in serious trouble without a national government in place to assist them. Further, to effectively deal with what big business, particularly the oil industry and agricultural companies like Monsanto, has done to the environment requires a national level of mobilization on the same level as was done during World War II. Sadly, the opportunity to have such a government has been lost over the years through deep level corruption, huge lobbying agendas, and a lack of regulation.

Now consider the double minus space, the authoritarian quadrant of our four-fold cultural compass. Authoritarians emphasize hierarchy. They tend to be more aggressive toward people who are different. That difference might be ethnicity, social class, sexual orientation, skin color, or religion, depending on the social context. In both libertarianism and authoritarianism, the focus is on how people differ in a competitive world (libertarian), or in a hierarchical society (authoritarian). Authoritarians direct hostility downward in the hierarchy ("kiss up, kick down") or outward toward some designated enemy that is outside the boundary or "beyond the pale." There is obeisance to higher ups if they are established authorities. Clearly authoritarian modalities increase through fear, a process well explored by Karen Stenner.[172]

The other two modalities of social relations, being more affiliative, tend to minimize social differences. But only one, the egalitarian modality, combines both high community affiliation with high autonomy for everyone, regardless of economic differences.

In all, authoritarianism with its double negative (for autonomy and affiliation) is the most dangerous one, at least for long-term sociocultural well-being. But a double negative doesn't necessarily imply that there is no affiliative behavior. Affiliation might exist for the people with whom they identify. For instance, the bonds created under battle or shared stress can be especially strong. Consequently, authoritarianism may have had its survival value in a tribal past during short-term sporadic conflicts. However, even then, conflict extending over years is physiologically destructive to the individual because of the toll taken on body and brain through constant high levels of cortisol and catecholamine.

There is one final point to make about the social realm. There are rogue individuals of a special type—extending along a continuum from narcissistic or borderline personality types to sociopathic/psychopathic types—where at the extreme end, there seems to be a total lack of conscience. To make up for that lack, there appears to be an ego motivated by strong power needs. I describe them as social dominators along the lines of Sidanius and Pratto, which has been acknowledged by that terminology in many subsequent papers.[173] The more successful sociopathic types among these unfortunates mask their deficiencies well. They are often quite charming and can gear and modulate their need for social power for the long run. They tend to be chameleon-like in that they will take on

the colors of whatever corporation, religion, or other group they target as
an opportunity in which to work up to a leadership position. These are
the types (not to mention agents provocateurs) who can be problematic
for nascent Occupy groups, where trust is so crucial. Dominators usually do best for themselves by allying with authoritarian groups, like fundamentalist religions that seek strong leaders and where their authority
is less likely to be questioned. I mention social dominators because they
can work parasitically in any one of the quadrants of the social realm,
though with most deadly effect in the authoritarian quadrant because that
is where they find people who usually do not question authority.[174]

A somewhat speculative thought concerns neoliberal ideology (an
Orwellian term that does not mean "liberal" in the usual sense of the
word).[175] The results of neoliberal policies in countries around the world
are extremely negative. Neoliberal agendas have been likened to piracy,
taking advantage of disasters in order to gain control over populations and
milking the financial coffers dry until the country finds itself in still worse
shape. Such policies are devastating. Naomi Klein's *The Shock Doctrine:
The Rise of Disaster Capitalism* describes the process in detail.[176] One of the
best ethnographic approaches in recent years is by anthropologist Janine
Wedel. Her book describes a new type of person—or power broker—she
calls a flexian. Flexians operate among the interstices of government and
business and are often above the law. They sound like what I would clas-
sify as a type of social dominator. Their modus operandi would explain
why it is so difficult to place them on the cultural compass. However, they
seem to be closest to the libertarian space. Wedel describes them as "the
world's new power brokers" who undermine democracy, government, and
the free market."[177]

Today, we see how a Berlin-Paris axis of (private) central banks has
reduced Greece to a shambles. If I were to choose a modalities quadrant
for neoliberals, the neoliberal agenda might fit least poorly in the competitive quadrant, the quadrant most characteristic of libertarianism.
In such a role, the privatization of public ownership (usually going to
wealthy cronies) becomes a strong agenda in a world where one percent

of the population commands enormous financial power. In a situation of economic depression and misery, all that financial power is looking for a way to commandeer whatever is left of value in a society, usually publicly-owned enterprises like water distribution, public lands for parks and conservation, or public schools. So, as more wealth becomes unequally distributed in a society, one moves into a new kind of class bifurcation reminiscent of feudalistic times. There is a mad scramble among the wealthy to take over whatever remains of the public wealth while reducing wages even further among an already depressed population. That is the neoliberal agenda currently in process. If unchecked, the ultimate outcome would be disastrous even without energy loss or the gathering storms of global warming. Disaster would already be at hand in an economic Armageddon, with no opportunities for amelioration in sight. Consequently, when energy loss and global warming eventually accelerate, many will lack the resilience to survive.

As fossil fuels become scarcer and more expensive, our laboratories will have to make adjustments, but scientific knowledge won't be lost. Dissemination of that knowledge can occur at much reduced costs. Nutritional understandings will greatly extend human productive lives, and digital technology will be improved at the nano-scale level. So, if we can reduce financial piracy and freeloading, elect corruption-free legislatures in honest elections, and obtain administrative and judicial bodies that serve the people, we might just succeed in escaping the worst of the storm clouds gathering over the planet. Here the transition movement, if it gains headway, can help move us toward a place with greater focus on community and local participation.[178] That would be the time for a new and more comprehensive level of understanding. And with that new understanding and its accompanying wisdom, we would find that life is better and more rewarding without a media-manipulating consumer culture that drains energy away from the rewards of higher education and the increased neuronal growth that accompanies it. With education, more energy can go into the third realm of cultural development, the symbolic realm. I haven't described that realm here, but it could involve a blossoming of art, music, literature, performances, and a science-based spirituality as we create a more rewarding lifestyle in local community.

In summary, we are better off thinking about how situations and policies can be measured and judged by our most recent understandings of the human sciences than by ideologies that score low in adaptive potential. Hopefully, the quadrants of the easy-to-use cultural compass will help us navigate through the ideologies and special interests that clutter up the media. Any policy, agenda, or ideology that lacks affiliation (in the social realm) and diversity (in the biomaterial realm) is likely to result in lower levels of cultural health. The cultural compass is one way to assess levels of affiliation and diversity in order to make decisions that promote a healthy culture and society.

NOTES

143 Huxley, Aldous. *The Perennial Philosophy.* (1st ed.) London: Chatto and Windus, 1946.

144 As quoted by Brown, Ellen Hodgson. *The Web of Debt:The Shocking Truth About Our Money System and How We Can Break Free,* 4th revised and expanded ed. Baton Rouge, LA: Third Millenium Press, 2010, p. 63.

145 Ibid.

146 For example, the Cato Institute, originally the Charles Koch Foundation where David Koch serves on the board. Koch once served as the Libertarian Party's official candidate for the U.S. Vice President. He continues to support the evisceration of government and its corporate regulatory functions, taxes, and supports the discrediting of climate warming, which is now a fully established scientific finding

147 Edelman, Gerald M. *Neural Darwinism : The Theory of Neuronal Group Selection.* New York: Basic Books, 1987.

148 Hebb, Donald O. *The Organization of Behavior, a Neuropsychological Theory.* New York: Wiley, 1949.

149 Forgays, Donald.G. and J.W. Forgays. "The Nature of the Effect of Free-Environmental Experience in the Rat." *Journal of Comparative Physiological Psychology.* 1952. p. 45.

150 Rosenzweig, M.R., E.L. Bennett, and D. Krech. "Cerebral Effects of

Environmental Complexity and Training among Adult Rats." *Journal of Comparative Physiological Psychology*. 1964. No. 57.

151 Whitbourne, Susan K. "Openness to Experience, Identity Flexibility, and Life Change in Adults." *Journal of Personality and Social Psychology*. 1986. Vol. 32, pp. 329–337.

152 Diamond, Marian Cleeves. *Enriching Heredity: The Impact of the Environment on the Anatomy of the Brain*. New York: The Free Press, 1988.

153 Ibid.

154 This is mere speculation. Its testing would depend upon a complex set of measuring indices as yet undeveloped.

155 See *Spirit Level*. Based on regression analysis from a sample of 40 nations used by Wilkinson and Pickett. I have left out Singapore, a city-state, for its small size and atypicality. It is the only nation in the list that is below the U.S. in rank.

156 *Spirit Level*, p. 19.

157 Ibid.

158 Inhofe's reason in an interview with Brad Johnson was that only God can change the climate, "The arrogance of people to think that we, human beings, would be able to change what He is doing in the climate is to me outrageous." As Johnson points out, "In the interview, Inhofe did not mention he has received *$1,352,523* in campaign contributions from the oil and gas industry, including $90,950 from Koch Industries." There are numerous internet references to this interview, see especially the twist that came to light in Rachel Maddow's interview where Inhofe said he used to believe in global warming until he found out the costs involved. thinkprogress.org/tag/climate-change-deniers/page/3/

159 Twenge, Jean. *Generation Me*. New York: Simon & Schuster, 2006.

160 *Spirit Level*, p. 45.

161 Bob Altemeyer's *The Authoritarians* is the most up-to-date and valuable book anyone can read, given our current predicament. He has done a prodigious amount of research, all cogently described with some healthy bits of humor here and there in earlier books. However, his best and latest book is available free to download on the Internet or for a nominal cost on paper. members.shaw.ca/jeanaltemeyer/drbob/TheAuthoritarians.pdf

162 Actually the measures of trust taken as an indicator by Wilkinson and Pickett were derived from answers to questionnaires also.

163 Colby, Benjamin N. "Well-Being: A Theoretical Program." *American Anthropologist.* 89: 4, 1987; Colby, Benjamin N. "Toward a Theory of Culture and Adaptive Potential." *Human Complex Systems. Mathematical Anthropology and Culture Theory: An International Journal.* 1: 3, 2003; Colby, Benjamin N., Kathryn Azevedo, and Carmella C. Moore. "The Influence of Adaptive Potential on Proximate Mechanisms of Natural Selection." *Mathematical Anthropology and Culture Theory: An International Journal.* 1: 3, 2003.

164 Colby, Benjamin N. and Pierre L. van den Berghe. *Ixil Country: A Plural Society in Highland Guatemala.* Berkeley: University of California Press, 1969.

165 Ibid.

166 A special case would figure in a more nuanced evolutionary theory, but I leave that aside for the moment.

167 Skeels, H.M. "Adult Status of Children with Contrasting Early Life Experience." *Monographs of the Society for Research in Child Development* . 31: 3, 1966.

168 Spitz 1945, 1946a, 1946b.

169 Montagu, Ashley. *Touching; the Human Significance of the Skin,* Third revised edition. New York: Harper and Row, 1986, p. 293.

170 Ainsworth, Mary D. Salter, and others. *Patterns of Attachment: A Psychological Study of the Strange Situation.* Hillsdale, N.J.: Lawrence Erlbaum Associates, 1978. Bowlby, John. *Attachment and Loss,* 2nd ed. London: Hogarth Press, Institute of Psycho-Analysis, 1982.

171 Chomsky, Noam. *Chomsky on Anarchism.* Oakland, California: AK Press, 2005; Graeber, David. *Fragments of an Anarchist Anthropology.* Chicago: Prickly Paradigm Press, 2004.

172 Stenner, Karen. *The Authoritarian Dynamic,* Cambridge: Cambridge University Press, 2005.

173 See: Altemeyer, Bob. *The Authoritarians.* Winnipeg: Bob Altemeyer, 2006. Available for download without cost.

174 This relationship of social dominators to authoritarians is cogently explained, based on empirical work, by Altemeyer, see *The Authoritarians.*

175 Except perhaps in economics where the word applies to those who believe in the specious concept of free markets and seek to avoid consumer protection laws or worker safety regulations by minimizing government and taxes to support themselves—a very different sense of "liberal."

176 Klein, Naomi. *The Shock Doctrine: The Rise of Disaster Capitalism.* New York: Metropolitan Books/Henry Holt, 2007.

177 Taken from the subtitle of Wedel, Janine R. *Shadow Elite.*

178 Hopkins, Bob. *The Transition Handbook: From Oil Dependency to Local Resilience.* White River Junction, VT: Chelsea Green Publishing, 2009; Hopkins, Rob. *The Transition Companion: Making Your Community More Resilient in Uncertain Times.* White River Junction, VT. Chelsea Green Publishing, 2011.

ABOUT THE AUTHORS

Ben Boyce

Ben has engaged in social and economic justice work since his youth in Tucson, Arizona. He has been active in supporting workers' rights through generating community support for progressive public policy initiatives and for union organizing campaigns around the county. He writes a regular column for the *Sonoma Valley Sun* newspaper and frequently appears on the Op-Ed pages of regional newspapers, where he serves as a consistent voice for economic and social justice. His past positions include serving as director of the Living Wage Coalition (2008–2011), a nonprofit advocacy organization focused on labor rights, quality jobs, and living wage policies. More recently, he served as the coordinator of the Accountable Development Coalition (ADC), a non-profit policy advocacy group in Sonoma County, which sponsors policy advocacy and public education on high-road economic and sustainable development strategies

Benjamin "Nick" Colby, Ph.D.

Ben received a B.A. with high honors from Princeton University, served for two years as an engineering office in the Navy, and received a Ph.D. in anthropology through the School of Social Relations at Harvard University. He taught in the Department of Social Relations at Harvard and in the Department of Anthropology at the University of California, Irvine. He has published in *Science*, *The American Anthropologist*, and other journals. Later as emeritus professor, he helped form the Social Dynamics and Complexity group at the Institute for Mathematical Behavioral Science at UC Irvine. Currently, he is working in agricultural anthropology at Swallow

Valley Farm at Valley Ford, California (www.swallowvalleyfarm.com). His most recent publication is "Narrative, Mind and Culture" in *A Companion to Cognitive Anthropology* (Blackwell and John Wiley & Sons, 2011).

Gus diZerega, Ph.D.

Gus holds a Ph.D. in political science from UC Berkeley. He successfully financed his dissertation as an artist businessman selling his art throughout the U.S. He is the author of several books and many articles and chapters on politics, ecology, and spirituality. He has taught at universities internationally, organized international scholarly conferences, and given workshops in healing, earth spirituality, and public events in the U.S. and Canada. Gus continues to be active in scholarly publishing in political and environmental theory. He is the author of *Power, Politics, and Persuasion: A Theory of Democratic Self-Organization* and is founding editor of the online open source academic journal *Studies in Emergent Order*.

Georgia Kelly

Georgia is the founder and director of Praxis Peace Institute. She has created multi-day conferences on peace-related themes and has organized several seminars at the Mondragón Cooperatives in Spain. She has also convened think tank projects for Praxis that focused on topics from species extinction to the 2011 pamphlet, "Deconstructing Libertarianism." She teaches conflict resolution and has enjoyed a successful career as a recording artist (harpist and composer), launching her own record label in 1978. A long-time active citizen, Georgia has chaired and co-chaired many issue-based political organizations and has worked on national and local candidate campaigns. She writes a blog for *The Huffington Post*.

Julianne E. Maurseth, Ph.D.

Julianne is a professor in the Green MBA program at the School of Business and Leadership at Dominican University (CA) and is president of Awake at Work, a consulting firm dedicated to bringing conscious choice to work. She has more than twenty years of management experience and conducts seminars in leadership development, communication skills, team building, and conflict resolution to professional organizations and corporations. Previously, she taught at Pepperdine University, Claremont University, and CSU Northridge. She was also an educational consultant and facilitator at the Museum of Tolerance in Los Angeles. Julianne has served on many boards, including the Olive View-UCLA Medical Center Foundation, and she currently serves on the board of Praxis Peace Institute.

Barry Spector

Barry writes about American history and politics from the perspectives of myth, indigenous traditions, and archetypal psychology. He has published articles in *Jung Journal: Culture and Psyche* and is the author of *Madness at the Gates of the City: The Myth of American Innocence* (Regent Press, 2010), which has received the PEN/Oakland 2011 Josephine Miles Literary award. He holds a B.A. from Harvard and has lectured at Sonoma State University and at the Institute for Transpersonal Psychology. Barry and his wife Maya present Oral Traditions Poetry Salons in their home and perform in the Great Night of Rumi poetry events.

PRAXIS PEACE INSTITUTE

PRAXIS PEACE INSTITUTE is a non-profit peace education organization dedicated to deep inquiry, creative problem solving, and informed civic participation. It is based in Sonoma, California.

In bringing together leading educators, researches, activists, and elected representatives, Praxis Peace Institute has established itself as a vehicle for practical workshops, cutting-edge conferences, and civic education. Our goal is to understand the failed mechanisms of the old systems in order to nurture the visions and alternative structures that support the evolution of systemic peace, social justice, and responsible stewardship of our planet.

Since its founding in 2001, Praxis Peace Institute programs have addressed the most relevant social challenges of our time. These areas include workshops in communication and conflict transformation, inquiries into the effects of culture and propaganda, conferences on participatory democracy and peace building, an invitational conference on solutions to species' extinctions, and a conference that explored what an economic system that supported peace would look like.

In addition to these programs, Praxis Peace Institute has also organized seminar/tours to the Mondragón Cooperatives in Spain and supports the model of worker-ownership as an economic model that supports peaceful relationships.

For information on our programs and events, please visit our website, www.praxispeace.org.

CPSIA information can be obtained at www.ICGtesting.com
Printed in the USA
LVOW05s1741191213

366070LV00034B/2192/P